Praise for *Truths from the*

"I've known Tina both personally and professionally for several years and have witnessed her grow as a leader, lecturer, and practice administrator. I personally endorse *Truths from the Trenches* as a must-read for any medical practice. Read this book and learn from one of the best."

~**Karen M. Keathley**, PMAC, PRAC
Executive Director, American Society of Podiatric Medical Assistants

———

"Reading this book, you may find yourself getting jealous that you don't have the 'perfect' manager. If that's the case, you have two choices: You can hire someone who checks all of Tina's boxes regarding what an effective manager looks like. Or you can buy this book for your current manager, yourself, and others on your team who take on a managerial role. Tina has provided you the guide to elevate your practice.

I highly endorse *Truths from the Trenches*. I will be buying copies for my team, and I invite you to do the same."

~**Dr. Andrew Schneider**, Vice President,
American Academy of Podiatric Practice Management

———

"I met Tina over fifteen years ago at a podiatry conference in Boston. I admired her for her calming personality and words of wisdom. She became my mentor when I joined the Executive Board of the American Society of Podiatric Medical Assistants (ASPMA). Lecturing across the country became our passion, and Tina was awe-inspiring.

I look forward to sharing her book and bringing new pearls of wisdom back to my office."

~**Nancy E Diaz**, MBA, RT, MRSO

"As a practice consultant, a challenge I often encountered was that the success—or failure—of my project was highly dependent on the motivation and competency of the office manager. My expertise was in efficiency techniques, not in motivating and supervising staff. Fortunately, Tina Del Buono has written *Truths from the Trenches*, a complete guide written to address this specific issue.

If you're a doctor who wants to improve your practice, this book will help you find the right office manager—one who will help you create an exceptional work environment."

~**Jon A. Hultman**, DPM, MBA, CVA

Author, *Reengineering the Medical Practice, The Medical Practitioner's Survival Handbook*

●———●———●

"Finally—the book that doctors and their managers have been searching for! *Truths from the Trenches* is exactly what it purports to be: true stories that happen to all of us practically every day; yet it is so much more. Tina not only describes the challenges faced by managers and their doctor employers, she also shares her wisdom and very practical advice about how to solve those problems.

Steeped in real-life systems and how-to-get-things-done examples, this book is a treasure. Read this book carefully, study it with your management team, and you cannot fail. Bravo!"

~**Rem Jackson**, CEO, Top Practices

●———●———●

"Tina distinguishes herself with *Truths from the Trenches: The Complete Guide to Creating a High-Performing, Inspired Medical Team*. Whether you're a member of a healthcare team and aspire to become an exceptional manager or you're a physician eager to recruit and train an administrator or manager, this book is a must-read. It outlines a precise strategy for taking your practice and its organizational and operational design to new heights. Your entire team should read this book."

~**John V. Guiliana**, DPM, MS
Executive Vice President, NEMO Health

●——●——●

"I had a great experience consulting with Tina to help coach my managers. She did a fantastic job of teaching them to effectively lead our staff to be more productive, organized, and pleasant. This book contains the valuable pearls and practical steps from someone who's been in the trenches and can transform your practice from good to great. This book is a must-read and should be used daily in your practice."

~**S. Don Kim**, DPM, ND, FACFAS

●——●——●

"This book is an absolute must-read for any new or established health team member, whether you're a medical office manager or any other staff member. Tina Del Buono has written a cheerful and wonderful guide to creating a great medical team. I only wish that these clear and helpful directions had been available when I started my practice forty-four years ago. A really easy and delightful read!"

~**Dan Fulmer**, DPM

●——●——●

"Many people want to be seen and even celebrated as an expert, and others are experts. That's Tina Del Buono. *Truths from the Trenches*, so aptly named, is packed with critical information and tactics that will lay your practice management challenges to rest forever. Read it, but more importantly, apply these truths."

~**Jay Henderson,** Real Talent Hiring

"Every doctor who owns a practice must gift this book to their office manager or administrator. No one is a born leader. You need a person who has great leadership skills to get your staff to work as a team with a common purpose. This book provides the tools administrators need to orchestrate a fine-tuned organization."

~**Dr. Peter Wishnie**, CEO of Family Foot & Ankle Specialists
Author, *The Podiatry Practice Business Solution*

●———●———●

"As a relatively new physician and private practice owner, I can say that *Truths from the Trenches* is worth more than gold! We invest so much in our medical education and then forget to educate ourselves about how to run a thriving practice. Tina Del Buono provides just that. Physicians can't afford NOT to read this book because it provides the map and catalyst for the foundation of a successful practice, and an even better one where the entire team enjoys coming to work. Thank you, Tina, for these priceless pearls of knowledge and for being bold enough to be transparent."

~**Marizeli Olacio**, DPM, Owner, Omega Medical Group in Miami, FL
Clinical Instructor at Barry University

●———●———●

"*Truths from the Trenches* is a must-read and an excellent resource for any office or practice manager. Tina has managed to put her twenty-four years of hands-on experience into a comprehensive, highly informative, and very thoughtful read. Her insights, powerful lessons, and solutions provide valuable real-life advice and encouragement for any medical practice or office manager."

~**Tressa R. Harvey**, PMAC, Practice Manager, Speaker

"Tina has been my friend, colleague, and mentor for the past seventeen years. She has an exceptional ability to bridge theory and actual real-world implementation of practice management. I've witnessed Tina's positive impact in helping healthcare professionals excel at any level, whether they are ancillary staff, management, or physicians. She possesses a marvelous ability to assess situations and process multiple social and business variables before recommending a solution. I trust and value her tremendously as a leader and mentor."

~**Jesus C. Vazquez**, PMAC

•———•———•

"Tina has been in my community for over twenty years. It's remarkable to see the passion she has toward making the office a productive, supportive, and fun environment for each member of the team. She is a well-respected educator and mentor for office managers and staff of every level. Her experiences and insights are invaluable to any practice."

~**Dr. Thomas J. Chang**, Redwood Orthopedic Surgery Associates

•———•———•

"Those of us who have been in practice for any length of time know how absolutely critical good staff, good communication, and camaraderie are to making the clinical experience great, not just for our patients, but for those of us in practice. Ms. Del Buono brings a wealth of experience to our field and is happy to share that wealth with all of us through this amazing book. This is a must-read for doctors, staff, and anyone working in the medical field."

~**Michael King**, DPM, FACFAS, FASPS

"Tina will help you learn about yourself, learn the ins and outs of how to become a successful leader, and learn how to inspire yourself and your team. Thank you, Tina, for your knowledge and for helping people be successful."

~**Shirley Traviss**, Practice Manager, Wilks Advanced Foot Care

———•——•——•———

"I've worked with Tina for many years at various practice management seminars. Her dedication to teaching staff—and doctors—to improve office functionality is amazing. This book is a must-have, especially in today's topsy-turvy environment."

~**Tony Poggio**, DPM

Truths

from the

Trenches

Truths

from the

Trenches

The Complete Guide to Creating
a High-Performing,
Inspired Medical Team

TINA DEL BUONO

Stonebrook Publishing
Saint Louis, Missouri

STONEBROOK
PUBLISHING

A STONEBROOK PUBLISHING BOOK
Copyright ©2021 Tina Del Buono

Library of Congress Control Number: 2021900222

ISBN: 978-1-7358021-4-5

www.stonebrookpublishing.net

PRINTED IN THE UNITED STATES OF AMERICA

10   9   8   7   6   5   4   3   2   1

Dedication

THIS BOOK IS DEDICATED to my husband John. Without your blind trust in a woman who had no management experience, I would never have had this amazing experience of over two decades of lessons learned in a medical practice.

I also thank my special travel buddy, Sue Bredekamp, for the many leadership and professional lessons I learned from her experiences over many a glass of wine on our travels.

And to my beautiful Aunt Dollie, who helped me see all of the beautiful lessons in life through her example as a teacher and mentor to me.

Contents

Introduction

I ALWAYS WANTED TO WORK in the medical field, and the opportunity came up a few years after I became a transcriptionist for a physician. He was shorthanded and needed a part-time back office person.

I jumped at the opportunity to help others and work side-by-side with a physician. While I looked forward to learning about patient care, I had no idea what was in store for me at my new job. Through a series of unfortunate events over the next two months, the doctor terminated his manager of ten years. Coming from a family of entrepreneurs, I jumped at the opportunity to step in as the manager when he asked.

The next few years were full of trials and many errors. Though I had run my own small home business for fifteen years and had three children, I'd never managed someone else's business or employees.

Over the past twenty-four years, I've immersed myself in hundreds of books, lectures, seminars, online courses, and podcasts to learn whatever I could to improve my management, coaching, and leadership skills. For the past seventeen years, I've had the opportunity to lecture nationally and internationally to physicians and their medical staff on Practice Management and Leadership topics.

A manager can either make or break a workplace, and the business owner usually finds this out too late. My goal is to help physician business owners and their management staff do one of two things:

1. Realize you don't have the skills or desire to be the best manager your employer has ever had and back away from the position
2. Realize that being a manager is your passion, and you're willing to invest in the time, trials, and training it takes to become the best manager your employer has ever had

If number 2 resonates with you, then you're reading the right book. Here's the first thing you need to know: you're responsible for your own personal growth.

It took me a few years to figure that out, but after I had a few failures, humiliations, and strained relationships, I took charge of my life and decided to learn how to become the person I wanted to be. I wanted to be a better person, a better partner, a better manager. And no one else could do it for me. It wasn't easy, and I had a few bumps along the way, but I figured it out through trial and error. Now I want to spare you that learning curve. So, I'm sharing some sound tools and principles about how you can live and work and enjoy the people you see every day—no matter how different or difficult they may be.

> Here's the first thing you need to know:
> you're responsible for your own personal growth.

I'd been managing a medical practice for a couple of years before I realized that I had very little knowledge about how people worked, how they developed their thought processes, and why they didn't do what I expected them to do. I knew how to manage clients and myself, but before now, the only other people I'd managed were my children. Turns out, I needed some help with my people skills.

At the time, three of us worked in the office with the doctor. My new front office assistant was delightful. She was smart and had a great personality but didn't have any medical office experience. I figured between my other experienced staff members and me, we'd be able to teach her. And we did.

She had no trouble doing her job tasks; the problem was how I gave her the tasks she needed to do each day. I'd developed a system that used a stacking file folder holder. There were three folders: one for her inbox, one for her outbox, and one for the problems she needed help with. It seemed simple and straightforward to me.

Each morning before she arrived, I would put the tasks she needed to complete in her inbox with a sticky note that said what needed to be done. Throughout the day, I added to her box. If she had a problem, she put it in her problem basket, and I would either fix it or put a note on it that told her how to do so.

After a few weeks, I noticed that whenever I put something in her basket, she'd make a sound under her breath—like you do when you're disgusted with something. At first I wasn't concerned, but it continued and I noticed that she became less interactive with me throughout the day. I thought I better ask her about it.

Boy, did I get an earful! Even though she knew the system, she didn't like the fact that I would dump work in her box without telling her what it was or asking her if she had any questions. I was shocked by her response and how upset she was about it. *How can she feel like she's having work dumped on her when this is her job?* I thought.

As we talked, it became evident that it wasn't so much the work that bothered her; it was that I didn't talk to her about the work. Giving her written notes made her feel disconnected from me, her manager. She needed more from me to feel a part of the work team.

Wow. I felt like I'd let us both down. I wondered how I could have prevented such an unpleasant experience for both of us. This was a valuable lesson that opened my eyes to how much I needed to learn to be a good manager.

Perhaps you need to learn better people skills too. Some call these "soft skills," but there's nothing soft about them. They're the most important skills you can develop to have a satisfying life, not just a satisfying career. And it's not like getting a college degree, where you reach the end and you graduate. You must grow, adapt, and hone your people skills every single day.

As a manager, you can never stop learning and cultivating these skills. You must have the desire and passion to learn how to be the best manager you can, so you can serve those you lead in an ethical and inspiring way.

I've been in a management position for over two decades now, and I've made most of the mistakes that a manager could. Some have been painful, but for the most part, they've been enlightening because I chose to learn from them.

Learning from your mistakes is the best education you can get. There's no better teacher than personal experience. When I think of my own mistakes, there are three primary reasons why I made them:

1. I thought that because I was in a management position, I had to have all the answers. I knew I didn't, but I thought I should.

2. I didn't take the time to look at the big picture when it came to making changes in the office. Change is difficult, at best, for most employees. I didn't take that into consideration.

3. I wasn't specific enough in my communication with staff members. And that's simply not fair. No one can read my mind, and they can't guess what I'm thinking.

Now I know better, and I truly love going to work each day—and it's not because there are no problems in my practice. It's because I know that I can handle whatever situations come up. My goal is to make our workplace a great place for everyone. I work for my coworkers. I freely share my knowledge, so they can understand how and why we do what we do, what the expectations are, and what happens if we fail to meet them. My coworkers are my first priority, and they know it.

> Our workplaces are only as good as the people who work there, and education and caring are the keys to making a practice the best it can be.

When I hire someone new, he or she is onboarded in a way that makes it clear that we appreciate them and want to help them learn and grow. The entire team helps with training. We are equals; no one is above or below another. Even though we may have different job tasks, they all connect together.

I love to hear patients comment to my coworkers, "You all seem so happy." I especially love to hear the reply, "That's because we love what we do!" Our workplaces are only as good as the people who work there, and education and caring are the keys to making a practice the best it can be.

So, I pass along these lessons, the pearls in my treasure chest, to you. Although this book is small, its impact can be huge. It's up to you!

Chapter 1

How to Find
the Right Manager

*Every minute devoted to putting the
proper person in the proper slot is worth
weeks of time later.*
~ Coleman Mockler, former CEO of Gillette

D R. JOHNSON WAS SHOCKED when his office manager, Nancy, gave her two-week notice. She'd been with
him since he started his practice ten years earlier. At first, it
had been only him, Nancy, and one other part-time employee.
Now his practice had grown to include two doctors and six
staff members in addition to Nancy. But Nancy's husband accepted a new position, and they were transferred to a town that
made it too far for her to commute.

Nancy knew everything about the practice. She'd worked
every position and had personally trained all the current staff
members. She was so good that she could anticipate what Dr.
Johnson and the practice needed, and she got everything done.

She was great with the staff and they loved working together. *No one*, he thought, *can replace Nancy.*

Two weeks! That wasn't nearly enough time to hire and train someone new. But since Nancy was so great, Dr. Johnson figured she must have written down their protocols and procedures that they could use to train a new manager. Not so. When he asked to see the office manuals, he was shocked that there were none.

Nancy kept everything in her head, rarely took a vacation, nor was she ever sick. She worked hard to keep all aspects of the practice workload up and current, even working on some weekends. She was great at teaching others what they needed to do, but she never thought about writing down the procedures and protocols for each position or what her own responsibilities were—including the systems she used to manage the office.

Dr. Johnson was sick about this situation. How could this have happened? What could he do to replace Nancy, whom he felt was irreplaceable? When she left the practice, all the know-how and management systems would walk out the door with her.

He didn't have time to post an ad to get someone to replace her. He needed someone immediately. Nancy promised to train her replacement, so they had to get started right away. He thought of Kathy, one of his back office medical assistants. He really liked her, and she'd been in the practice for three years. Kathy received instructions well and always exceeded the expectations of her job position. She was always at work on time, and the patients loved her.

Dr. Johnson also remembered that Kathy had been a medical receptionist prior to working in his practice. Ah, he thought, *She's trained in both the administrative and clinical aspects of a medical practice. She's perfect!*

Kathy was honored and somewhat shocked that Dr. Johnson offered her the office manager position because she'd never managed a medical practice—or any other type of business. He told her that she was a perfect fit for the position, and he was sure that she'd catch on to all the elements she needed to do the job.

But Kathy wasn't convinced. She'd only been in the practice for three years, and there were other staff members with more seniority. How would they react if she needed to confront them about mistakes? Would they listen to her ideas? Although she loved a challenge, she also loved being the back-office assistant and working closely with the patients and doctors.

Dr. Johnson was in a bad situation, and Kathy didn't want to make it worse for him or the practice, so she accepted the position. She hoped that Nancy would show her everything she needed to do. Right now, she had no idea what Nancy's job involved.

Nancy made a list of her job duties, and Kathy shadowed her as much as possible for the next two weeks. Since a back-office replacement had not yet been found, Kathy also had to fill in with her old job while trying to learn Nancy's job. She took precise notes but, ultimately, she knew there was no way she could learn everything that Nancy knew in only ten days. After all, Nancy had been in that position for ten years.

The two weeks flew by, and before they knew it, they were celebrating Nancy's departure. Kathy was quite nervous, and she told Nancy she didn't think she could do the job as well as she had. Nancy told her not to worry—everything would work out.

"If there's something you don't know how to do," Nancy said, "just ask Dr. Johnson."

All too soon, Kathy found out that there was a lot she didn't know. And the way she found out was when a problem came up that she didn't know how to handle, or she wouldn't have completed something the doctors wanted because she didn't know anything about it. Whenever she asked Dr. Johnson what to do, he told her to try to figure it out for herself because he was busy and the back office was shorthanded.

The situation got progressively worse. When they hired a new back-office medical assistant, guess who had to train her? Kathy. Every day that she was in the back training the new hire, everything she should have been doing in her new position was put on hold.

After a few weeks, Kathy came in on a Saturday—something she'd promised her husband she'd never do—to assess the situation of the office. She didn't even know where to begin. She was upset, sad, and angry. She felt that Dr. Johnson had lied to her when he said she'd be able to do the job. He never took the time to listen to her or offer his help.

She'd loved her job before Nancy resigned, but now she hated her situation. Instead of catching up on her work, she updated her resume so she could find a new job. After all, this was Dr. Johnson's problem, not hers.

So, what could Dr. Johnson have done to prevent this catastrophic event from happening? He could have taken the time to create reliable documentation, such as a job description that listed the details of the office manager's duties and tasks, including what systems he/she oversaw and how. It should have listed the expectations of the manager, who they oversaw, and what attributes and qualities the manager needed to have. Plus, the skills and experience that were required.

He also needed written protocols for every task the office manager performed, including monthly timelines that showed when each task was due. Having regular meetings between him and the office manager were crucial to avoid surprises, and the practice vision should have been kept current and out front for all to know.

Had Dr. Johnson had these things in place, he could have taken more time to search for the right person because he already had a "recipe" for what his office required. After the new person was hired, he or she would have all of the details of their job position and the protocols for the job tasks to follow.

> Had Dr. Johnson had these things in place, he could have taken more time to search for the right person because he already had a "recipe" for what his office required.

You, too, need to have this kind of documentation for every position in your practice, but especially for the office manager position because he or she oversees all the others. If you don't have a well-trained person in that position, you're setting your practice up for future difficulties and failures.

How to Find the Right Office Manager

Many physicians have had managers that didn't work out. The most common reason is because they hired someone who had no previous management experience or training, and the doctor thought that person could figure it out. Further, the doctors often didn't know what their new manager needed to do to excel in the position. In most of these unfortunate cases, the new hire didn't have a job description that detailed their duties or spelled out the protocols to follow in order to be successful. So, they did the best they could—and that wasn't good enough.

It's hard enough to hire the right person for any position in your practice, but when you're hiring someone to oversee the entire practice and make sure everything is done the way you want it to be done, it's extremely difficult.

Here are some things to consider before you place a hiring ad:

- Does the office require a full-time manager, or will the manager also hold another position in the practice; i.e., administrative or clinical staff position?
- How many staff members and physicians will the manager oversee?
- Will the manager be responsible for paying bills and doing payroll, or does an outside service do this?
- What are the exact job tasks and personnel the manager will oversee? These must be clearly spelled out.

Answering such questions will help you put together a list of skills and experience that are needed for an office manager.

Consider how many staff members and physicians are in your practice. The size of your staff can determine what education and experience level the office manager needs to make sure the practice not only runs well, but so it can grow. Your office manager doesn't always have to have a business degree. It depends on the specific job requirements.

Far too often, the person who's been with the practice the longest is fingered to fill the manager position. This isn't always a bad thing, but that person may not be prepared for or trained to take on the responsibilities and duties necessary to run a successful practice. Even though this might seem like the right person for the job, if he or she doesn't have the skills to manage the practice, you're setting them up for failure. They must be intentionally trained for their new position to be successful. If selecting this person is your knee-jerk response, your practice will inevitably lose employees, patient growth, revenue, and time—none of which can ever be regained. Filling this position must be done with much thought and care; choosing the wrong candidate can be disastrous.

> Far too often, the person who's been with the practice the longest is fingered to fill the manager position.

And yet, many very successful medical practices are managed by someone who's come up through the ranks. They knew the ins and outs of all the job positions and possessed the right people skills and vision to take the practice to the highest level of excellence. A manager mentor is a great option for providing the necessary training for a successful transition in such situations.

A manager mentor is someone who is managing a medical practice similar to yours. They understand how a successful practice is run. They help onboard a new manager and support them through the first several months of their new position.

When I became an office manager, I had no prior experience in the medical field, so I contacted two local managers who agreed to help me with what I needed for the first several months. I don't know what I would have done without their help and guidance. Now I offer this service through Top Practices. I help mentor and onboard new practice managers, so they can be successful in their new position and the practice can perform to the highest level of efficiency as they grow and learn. Everyone needs support when taking on a new position, and a manager mentor can help your new office manager grow in skills and confidence.

Create the Job Description

Most medical practices assign certain tasks to particular job positions. But they forget to write down what the office manager does, when it should be one of the first job descriptions they create. Once that position is defined, you can assign all the other job tasks to the other positions your practice requires.

A job description is a written statement that describe the following:

- The duties of the position
- What the person in this position is responsible for, to whom, and when
- Most important contributions and outcomes needed from the position
- Required qualifications and skill sets for the position
- The vision and environment of the practice

Your goal in hiring an office manager is to find the brightest, most competent, flexible, and reliable employee you can find. When you have a carefully-constructed job description, it helps you hire someone who's qualified to do the tasks the position requires. Before hiring, you must have a full understanding of the competencies and skills needed to fulfill those tasks.

To develop the job description, analyze the actual tasks your office manager performs. The description should clearly identify all responsibilities of this specific position and the most important outcomes for each specific job task. Include information about the working conditions, any tools and equipment that will be used, and the knowledge and skills the candidate must possess.

The job description is a living document that you'll update as the job responsibilities expand, which happens frequently in the medical field. It shouldn't limit the employee but allow him or her to stretch their experience, grow their skills, and develop their ability to contribute to the organization.

Job descriptions are an integral part of the performance development planning process for the office as a whole. The medical Office Manager position is critical to ensure that the overall business operations of the practice run smoothly and professionally.

A medical office manager's duty will vary according to the size of the medical practice. There are certain primary tasks and responsibilities that are common to all medical office manager positions.

Managing a medical office takes a diverse skill set that ranges from clerical to clinical, including understanding medical terminology, possessing accounting and bookkeeping skills, and possessing knowledge of clinical treatments and procedures.

Although the skills above are important, the most important skill an office manager must possess is people skills. The manager must be able to inspire the staff by communicating the purpose and the vision of the practice. The manager should be skilled at showing each staff member the role they play in the success of the practice.

> . . . the most important skill an office manager must possess is people skills.

No matter how much an office manager knows about how the medical practice must be run, if they cannot develop good relationships with the staff personnel and inspire them to perform at high standards, they will not be successful.

POSITION OVERVIEW:
Medical Officer Manager Job Description

Name: **Job Position:** Medical Office Manager
Hire Date:

Primary Essential Job Function:

The Medical Office Manager position is critical in ensuring that the overall business operations of the medical practice run smoothly and professionally. Managing a medical office takes a diverse skill set, from clerical to clinical.

The manager's duties will vary according to the size of the practice, but certain primary tasks and responsibilities are common to all medical office manager positions. The skills needed include understanding medical terminology, accounting and bookkeeping skills, and knowledge of clinical treatments and procedures.

Although these skills are important, the most important skills an office manager needs to possess are people skills. The manager must be able to inspire the staff and communicate the purpose and the vision of the practice, as well as stress the important role the staff plays in the success of the practice. No matter how much the office manager knows about how the medical practice must be run, if they cannot develop good relationships with the staff and inspire them to perform at high standards, they will not be successful themselves.

Job Tasks and Responsibilities:

- Hire and train, or oversee the training of, administrative and clinical staff
- Establish job descriptions and training protocols for staff
- Monitor and evaluate staff performance
- Establish office policies and oversee training the staff on them
- Ensure compliance with state healthcare regulations
- Manage insurance contracts
- Oversee patient scheduling
- Communicate with patients regarding inquires or complaints
- Ensure that patient records and documentation are accurately input into the software system
- Oversee billing and collection procedures to ensure that clean claims are processed and monies due to the practice are collected in a timely fashion
- Responsible for OSHA compliance
- Responsible for facility cleaning and waste management
- Oversee or perform inventory management and ordering of supplies
- Oversee or perform payroll duties
- Oversee or submit payroll taxes
- Ensure that all licensing and certifications are current for physicians and staff
- Oversee insurances for physician, staff, and facility

- Create and manage systems in the practice to ensure that all tasks are complete and correct
- Schedule office meetings, develop an agenda, and follow-up
- Have a full understanding of state employee law
- Ensure continuing education is provided for all staff members including the manager
- Provide a pleasant work atmosphere that employees enjoy

Training Required:	Completed Date:
Software:	
Computer skills:	
Communication skills:	
Leadership training:	
HR state training:	
OSHA compliance:	
Billing/Coding:	
State employment law:	
Risk management:	
State tax laws:	
Inventory supply:	
State insurance law:	
Insurance contracting:	

Job Task Training Log: Has completed and is fully competent in knowledge and skill to handle and oversee the following:

	Y/N Needs Training
Staff position responsibilities and protocols:	
Office patient flow with scheduling and time flow:	
Daily Revenue Sheet/Activity Report/Balancing:	
Employee policies and office manual:	
Accounts payables and receivable reports:	
Inventory supply requirements:	
Running effective office meetings:	
Understands and can teach OSHA compliance:	
Full understanding and knowledge of state employment law:	
Understands insurance contracting:	
Fully understands billing, coding and Explanation of Benefits:	
Developed continuing training program:	
Fully understands of risk management and training:	
Excellent communication skills:	
Develops "circular systems strategies" and accountability checks:	
Creates an environment that staff members like to work in:	
Has regularly scheduled report meetings with physician:	

Qualities of an Office Manager

The office manager must know and demonstrate the main purpose of their position: to ensure the staff is trained, happy, and understand the vision and purpose of the practice. They must be focused on the success of the practice as a whole.

Key competencies of a manager

- Good judgment
- High ethics and integrity
- Planning and organizational skills
- Attention to details
- Adaptability
- Customer service orientation
- Problem analysis and assessment
- Decision-making
- Maintains confidentiality
- Excellent communication skills
- Excellent stress management skills
- Capable of delegating authority and responsibility
- Resourceful information gathering and monitoring
- Excellent leadership skills
- Excellent coaching skills
- Excellent teamwork and collaboration skills

If your office manager doesn't have these skills and competencies, your practice will eventually suffer.

Finding the right office manager may be difficult. It takes time and effort to develop the job description that includes what the person needs to know, must be able to perform, and the qualities he or she needs to possess. Take your time before your hire someone. The wrong choice can be catastrophic for your practice.

Key qualities of a manager

Below are ten of the most sought-after qualities employers are seeking in management personnel. When you take each one at face value, they are very reasonable to attain, but so difficult to find in candidates. These qualities are not listed in any order:

- They care about the success of their team. It's not about them; their success is based on their team's success.
- They are always looking for those they can train up to become their successor when they leave.
- They possess great decision-making skills. They think things through and search for the best direction, keeping all persons in mind.
- They have a passion for creating a positive work environment for the team as a whole.
- They realize that they are as human as their teammates and, therefore, have weaknesses and faults.
- They have a vision of what their team is able to accomplish and seek to complete it.
- They are a leader and the gatekeeper and protector of their team.
- They are flexible. They realize that sometimes plan B or C may need to become plan A.
- Things happen, and they immediately move their team through it instead of wading into it.

- They possess good communication skills. To be understood and to have understanding are key points in creating connection between them and their team members.
- They display good ethics, high integrity, and live by the Golden Rule. They walk the talk and inspire their team members to be great!

Why is it so hard to find a manager with all these qualities? Perhaps it's not. It's all about the questions you ask during the interview.

Before you start interviewing, make a list of the characteristics and qualities that are important to you. During the interviews, keep that list in front of you and check off the skills and qualities the candidate displays. Be sure to take notes you can refer to later. When you're interviewing multiple people, it's easy to forget what you liked about the specific person and what the candidate had to offer.

> Before you start interviewing, make a list of the characteristics and qualities that are important to you.

Interview Questions

When interviewing for an office manager, you need to ask different questions than you would if you were hiring an administrative or clinical person. A managerial candidate must be able to communicate his or her skill set and experience during the interview.

The manager position impacts the whole office and, therefore, the entire staff. Picking the right person isn't easy, but there are some things you can do to make the decision less stressful and can help you avoid making a mistake.

My friend and colleague, Jay Henderson of Real Talent Hiring (www.RealTalentHiring.com) has a process for evaluating your candidates to help you in your decision making for this important position. It's called "The Hiring MRI Performance Assessment." Jay has helped hundreds of physicians place the correct candidate in their practice.

In his book *The Ultimate Small Business Guide to Hiring Super-Stars: A New Formula Guaranteed to Find the Right People For Your Business,* Jay explains the process he uses when interviewing candidates. He calls it the Four-Level Deep Questioning.

When you ask a question such as, "What do you think you will like the most about this job?" Jay suggests you take their answer and turn it in to the next level of questioning. Here's the example Jay uses in his book:

> Let's say the candidate answers the question above by saying, "I like the flexibility you described in the job posting." So, the next level of questioning would be, "What is it about flexibility that appeals to you?"
>
> Then the candidate replies, "I like that if my schedule changes and if I need to come in later, I would be able to adjust my time to come in, but stay later that day so that I get the same amount of hours in."
>
> The next level of question to follow-up on this issue might be, "Okay. Do you expect that your schedule will change often?"
>
> And the next level question might be, "Is there a potential of schedule conflict that we should be aware of?"

By using Jay Henderson's Four-Level Deep Questioning method, you can dig deeper into the questions you ask. You can also discover where the candidate may have potential conflicts with the job position.

The questions below can help pull this vital information from the candidate:

- How do you plan your daily, weekly, and monthly schedule so that you complete the job tasks necessary to running a medical practice?
- How do you set goals for yourself?
- How would you set goals for the staff members and practice?
- Describe the range of your responsibilities at your previous position.
- What goals did you set for yourself at your last position? How did you achieve them?
- What's your approach to conflict resolution? How has that approach worked out in the past?
- Describe what you would classify as an office crisis. How did you deal with it?
- How do you keep track of office resources?
- What did you do to ensure the security of patient office records at your last job?
- What administrative processes worked well at your last position?
- What new systems did you set up in your last position? How did they work?
- How do you implement changes in procedures or protocols with staff members?
- What's the most challenging thing about being an office manager?

- In what ways have you worked with your team to increase productivity?
- Describe your approach to conducting training sessions with employees.
- How have your previous employer/manager relationships been?
- Can you demonstrate how you would delegate a task to a staff member?
- What are your steps to solving a problem in the office?
- What have been your manager/leadership roles and experiences?
- Describe your management attributes.
- How do you reward staff for a job well done?

Of course, you'd like to get to know the candidate as much as possible before making a hiring decision. Jay suggests you make it a temporary hire if a key employee—like Nancy in Dr. Johnson's office—gives a two-week notice. Excellent idea! Then both parties can find out if it's a good match while the training and onboarding takes place. His or her performance, attitude, and skills can be assessed before you make a permanent decision.

Don't be in a hurry to hire your new office manager. Your practice is the financial lifeline for your family and those you employ. Although it's always inconvenient to take the time to search for the perfect person to manage your practice, it's more than worth it. Making a hasty decision only makes the process longer, more costly, and more painful.

> Don't be in a hurry to hire your new office manager.

Back to Dr. Johnson and Kathy. Kathy left her resignation letter—with all the details of her disappointment and anger—on Dr. Johnson's desk. When he arrived early on Monday morning, he felt sick when he read it.

He realized he'd made a mistake, not by offering Kathy the position because he still felt she would be great at the job, but because he hadn't known how to handle the situation when Nancy left. He'd simply hoped it would somehow work itself out.

When Kathy arrived, he apologized for the situation he'd put her in and how poorly he'd handled it.

"If I got you some help and training, would you consider staying?" he asked.

"I'd like that," Kathy answered. "I really enjoy working with you and the rest of the staff." She was happy that he cared enough about her to get her some help.

Dr. Johnson made calls to his physician friends to see if they knew of any resources to help in such a situation. He found out about a company that offered manager mentoring, and he called to make an appointment for that evening to find out the details. He asked Kathy to join him.

Over the next several months, Kathy received the training she needed. She learned the importance of being a practice manager and how she could set up systems and protocols for the practice by involving the entire team. Over the next several years, Kathy continued to have monthly check-ins with her mentor, and Dr. Johnson said it was the best investment he ever made. Not only did Kathy work out great, but the systems and protocols the team had set up in his practice would ensure that he'd never have this problem again. His practice was growing, and the people who worked with him were engaged and happy.

Chapter 2

Assess Yourself
as a Manager

Self-awareness is gained by self-evaluation.
If you want to be better aware of who you
are, where you can grow, how you can uniquely
give or serve, you need to evaluate yourself.
~ Brendon Burchard

IT SHOULD BE NO SURPRISE that there are many different management styles. Some styles seem to work better in certain situations than others, and some styles don't work well at all. Successful managers understand the different styles of managing and learn to use a little bit of this and a little bit of that, depending on the situation and the team member(s).

Take, for example, the Autocratic management style. Not too many people like working for a dictator, but in some cases, certain people need someone to "dictate" to them what needs to be done and how each aspect of the day must go. They like to know what's expected of them, and they feel secure with a manager who uses this style because they know what they need to accomplish to do their job well.

Then there are managers who follow a Democratic management style. They take time to understand the different points-of-view and get feedback from their employees, so they can make informed decisions. Unlike the Autocratic top-down management style where decisions are made by the manager, the Democratic management style encourages employee participation, which can create more openness between coworkers and foster a willingness to work together.

But my favorite is the Teamwork/Coaching management style where each person has certain tasks that they're accountable for, but they also interact well with each other and help one another as the needs arise. They work together for the common goal of the business and realize they're all in it together. "All for one and one for all" is the attitude. This type of manager is like a coach to the team members. The manager sees each person's strengths and weakness and encourages each one to be the best they can within their skill set. The manager also provides training, so each can grow in their position.

Whatever management style you use—or what blend of them—it must fit the practice's and staff members' best interests.

When I was a young manager, I always thought I had to know everything, so I could answer my staff's questions and tell them what needed to be done. After all, if I didn't know the answer, then why was I the manager? I always tried to stay one step ahead of everyone, which was really great from a learning and knowledge standpoint, but it was extremely difficult. If I was asked something I didn't know, I'd research the topic to find the answer.

One day, I shared this situation with one of my mentors. I mentioned how hard I had to study and research to make sure I knew all of the answers.

She said, "Why don't you tell them that what they asked was a great question and that you don't have the answer. Suggest that you find the answer together. If you don't allow others to participate in learning, they'll never grow or take a true interest in the practice."

What? I didn't need to know everything on the spot? What a relief! That's when I became more excited about mentoring my team. I asked them to research topics we needed to learn about or new systems we might use. This not only freed up my time, but my staff became engaged with their jobs and the business overall.

I'd been holding back my employees and myself from becoming better at what we each did. I'd been practicing the "I" not "we" method of managing, and it didn't work. If I wanted to grow as a manager, I had to allow my team to grow and, as a result, the practice would grow. The same is true for you.

> I'd been holding back my employees and myself from becoming better at what we each did.

I'm a firm believer that all managers must have a heart to mentor those they work with. When you mentor someone, you take him or her under your wing, and you invest in them, so they can grow and become more successful and valuable as a person and to the company. A great manager never holds an employee back from learning more, doing more, or being able to achieve more.

The better your staff performs and the more they enjoy their jobs, the better you can perform and grow as well.

Mentoring takes time, but its return is tenfold. Nothing makes most managers feel more successful than when their staff grows in skill and knowledge.

Below are five benefits of being a mentoring manager:

1. You create a caring and empowering relationship with your staff members.
2. You retain your employees. People don't leave jobs they like or where they feel valued.
3. Your load becomes lighter and more enjoyable.
4. Because of your positive reinforcement, your employees become willing to go the extra mile.
5. Mentoring drives loyalty to you and to the practice, which creates loyal customers.

Mentoring managers always look out for their employee's best interests and, in turn, their employees do the same for their manager and the business they serve.

Self-Evaluation: the Key to Becoming a Better Manager

As a parent, I learned a very valuable lesson, which I drew upon years later when I moved into a management position. Here it is: what worked with one child—whether it was discipline, motivation, or a teaching opportunity—didn't necessarily work for the next child.

All three of my children were, and are, very different from each other, and I had to find out what worked for each one. The same is true when managing staff. Because they're adults, they're a bit easier to read, but it's your job to figure out each one of them.

You must begin with a self-evaluation. This isn't always easy to do because as managers, you're so involved in every aspect of the practice that you may not see what's actually going on daily. Start by watching and listening to your staff members. How do they react when you interact with them? Are they comfortable? Do they smile at you? Do they feel free to ask questions or tell you when they make a mistake?

Ask yourself, *What type of relationship do I have with each of my staff members? What do I know about them, and do I really care about them?"* Evaluate yourself throughout the day and ask, "Would I like to be managed by me?"

The office manager position can be very difficult, and at times, your staff may think you can make decisions about work issues on the spot when you cannot. You not only work closely with your staff members, but you also answer to and work closely with your physician employers. It can feel like you get tossed back and forth between the two, and it can be quite a challenge.

> The office manager position can be very difficult, and at times, your staff may think you can make decisions about work issues on the spot when you cannot.

When you say you're going to do something for a staff member, do you do it? There's little that can sour relationships quicker than not keeping your commitments and following through on promises made. Do you make sure that your staff members know you have their backs and are watching out for them? Do they know you'll stand up for them when it's necessary and appropriate?

To evaluate yourself, ask yourself the following questions and answering them honestly. It will help you discover what you can improve to become a better manager. If the answer is *True*, ask yourself why it's true. List what you're do-ing right, and then write down how you could improve or change altogether.

- I believe I'm an effective manager. True or False
- My employees would say that I'm an effective manager. True or False
- I have confidence in my own abilities. True or False
- I understand what's expected of me. True or False
- My people clearly understand what's expected of them. True or False
- My attitude at work is positive. True or False
- I'm a good communicator; I listen and seek to under-stand. True or False
- I set an appropriate example for my staff. True or False
- I establish clear expectations for my staff, verbally and in writing. True or False
- My people feel good about working for me. True or False
- I look forward to coming to work in the morning. True or False
- I am effective in coaching my staff to higher levels of performance. True or False
- My biggest management challenge is:

_____

_____

_____

_____

_____

_____

_____

• My management strengths and weaknesses are:

_____

_____

_____

_____

_____

_____

• My staff would describe me as:

_____

_____

_____

_____

_____

_____

_____

- My four biggest management frustrations are:

_____

_____

_____

_____

_____

_____

- My management skill goals, and accomplishments for the next twelve months are:

_____

_____

_____

_____

_____

_____

When you're finished, set a time to talk through your answers with your physician employer to get their input. Then revisit the true/false section and rank them. Number your answers according to what would have the most impact if you improved in this area. You might find that by doing this, you will take care of some of your biggest frustrations.

Start ticking away at each issue that's holding you back from becoming the manager you want to be. Schedule time on your calendar to work on these areas, and search for books that address the topic you're working on. Don't forget to check YouTube for management videos—or contact me by email at gotoppm@gmail.com and I'll help you.

This kind of self-improvement takes time, but don't give up. As long as you're working on your list and are moving forward, that's success. In turn, if you don't have a plan to further your growth as a manager, it won't happen. It's up to you.

Are You the Manager Your Employer Wants?

Whether you're fortunate enough to be employed or are currently looking for employment, job security is different than it was in years past. The pool of eligible and highly qualified people is quite large, so it's imperative that you understand what employers want in prospective employees, as well as in the employees they already have. Stay at the top of your game.

Evaluating yourself as a manager will help you figure out how to manage the staff better. Knowing what your employer wants in a manager will help you figure out what areas you need to improve to be the best of the best at your job.

> Evaluating yourself as a manager will help you figure out how to manage the staff better.

Here's a list of the top seven non-negotiable attributes that employers seek in management and staff personnel:

1. They are ethical: Be a person who holds firm to the belief and practices of The Golden Rule: do unto others as you would have others do unto you. You can't go wrong if this is your ethical foundation. Integrity and accountability speak louder than any words. Make your yes mean yes and your no mean no. Always speak the truth.

It takes time to build trust with your employer, but once it's established, you must do everything you can to protect it. It's hard to repair broken trust, if it can be repaired at all.

A manager who has professional, ethical standards is highly valued in the workplace. They are also becoming rare. Be that person.

Sometimes people think their ethics can fall into a grey area and still be OK; I disagree, and here's a story to illustrate my point. Kristine had managed a large medical practice and was in charge of ordering the office supplies. There was a certain office supply chain that always offered bonus gifts if you purchased over a certain amount. They offered nice gifts like Fitbit step trackers, headsets, cell phone holders, weekly planners, gift certificates, etc.

Kristine always looked forward to the monthly catalog, so she could see what that month's gift was. She already had quite a collection of things from her purchases over the past few years. Kristine never thought that there was anything wrong with her taking the bonus gift each month; after all, it was free and didn't cost the practice anything. Until one day when her doctor asked her a question.

He saw a package on her desk with a pink Fitbit step tracker inside and said, "Hey, where did you get that? My wife has been wanting to get one."

For the first time, Kristine felt queasy in the pit of her stomach and said, "It was a free gift from the office supply store."

The doctor asked more questions about this free gift, and she explained how it worked: when they purchased items that exceeded a certain amount, a gift was included with their order. This led to a pretty long closed-door discussion later that day where Kristine had to tell the about all the "free gifts" she'd taken over the past few years.

"Why didn't you think that these gifts belonged to me, since the money to pay the bill came from my bank account?" the doctor asked.

"I guess I didn't think it was wrong because the gifts were free."

The doctor saw it much differently. This was one of those grey areas, at least in Kristine's eyes. After their talk, the doctor decided he would receive the free gift each month and then would use it as a prize for a fun raffle or marketing giveaway.

2. They are punctual: Arriving to work on time and being ready to work at the starting time are two totally different things. It's not enough to be in the building at the designated start of the day. Employers think you're on time if you've arrived in plenty of time to take care of whatever you need to before the designated starting time.; i.e., getting coffee, putting your personal items away, visiting the bathroom.

> Arriving to work on time and being ready to work at the starting time are two totally different things.

See the difference? Great employees arrive early and are ready to work on time.

Punctuality not only needs to be discussed when onboarding an employee, it needs to be documented in office Employee Manual and enforced. One of the best ways to enforce this is in the story of Bill, a back-office assistant for Dr. Dale.

Bill was a great employee. He always went above and beyond when it came to patient care, and his coworkers really liked him— except for one bad habit he had. Bill was always five to ten minutes late to work, but once he got there, he was a mover and shaker. Dr. Dale had heard the other staff members talking about this situation. They didn't think it was right that Bill could be consistently late but was never written up for it—especially because they were always on time. The office manager wanted to address this with Bill, but Dr. Dale was afraid that Bill might quit if he was written up, and he was really a great employee.

The office staff had a morning huddle every day with Dr. Dale to review the schedule and go over any problems of the previous day. They had to wait until Bill got there to start the meeting because he was the lead back-office assistant and needed to review the schedule for the day. All eight of the office staff and Dr. Dale waited five to ten non-productive minutes each morning until Bill arrived.

One day, a front-office staff member spoke up.

"Do you realize that you're losing money every day?" she asked Dr. Dale.

"What do you mean?" he asked.

"Well, there are eight people who wait five to ten minutes—and sometimes more—to start working every morning because Bill is tardy," she said. "I don't know how much everyone makes, but if you multiplied what you pay each person per minute and add up how many minutes we sit here waiting for Bill each day, I bet you'll find out that you've paid us a lot of money over a year for doing nothing."

Dr. Dale hadn't thought of that and was a bit embarrassed. He knew she was right and that no matter how good an employee Bill was, he was costing the practice money. That evening, Dr. Dale told the entire team, including Bill, that their morning huddle would begin at 8:00 a.m. sharp, and everyone needed to be there on time. The next morning, all the staff— with the exception of Bill—were there at eight o'clock. Instead of waiting, Dr. Dale started the meeting.

Everyone one was shocked and pleased, but no one was more shocked than Bill when he walked in late and the meeting was in progress. Bill felt uncomfortable because he didn't know what had been discussed, and he was one of the key back office players. He had to ask his coworker what he'd missed, and she wasn't really happy to stop and take the time to bring him up to speed.

The next morning the meeting started on time and, once again, Bill was absent. When he asked his coworker what had happened, she refused to tell him. Dr. Dale overheard the conversation and told Bill that he needed to be there for the meeting along with everyone else if he wanted to do his job to the best of his ability.

The next morning everyone was surprised when Bill arrived five minutes early and took his place at the meeting spot. A couple of coworkers even gave him a high five, and Dr. Dale said he was glad he made it on time.

Physician business owners and managers sometimes allow bad habits like tardiness to become acceptable, and they are not. When policies are in place, everyone must adhere to them for the practice to run efficiently. Everyone is held to the same standard.

3. They pay attention: One of my pet peeves is when a new or established employee doesn't take notes while they're learning something new, and they later ask someone for help because they don't remember how to do the task.

As the manager, whether you're asked to take notes or not, you should take notes. Unless you have a photographic memory, your notes will come in handy at some point. An employer translates not paying attention into a lack of initiative when it comes to your job education. They'll frown on you if you interrupt other employees and take up their time to help you with a task that you've been trained to do. To the employer, you're costing them additional money because they're now paying for the extra help you need.

> As the manager, whether you're asked to take notes or not, you should take notes.

Your employer notices when you don't pay attention to what's being taught and what's going on in the business. So, pay attention, take notes, and stay in a learning mode. You're the role model for the staff members you oversee.

I learned this lesson the hard way, and that's probably one of the reasons why written protocols and instructions are so important to me. I don't want any of my staff to feel the way I did when I was first hired to work in a medical practice. I was very "green," and the only medical background I had was being a medical transcriptionist. I could type every medical term conceivable, but I had no idea what most of them meant.

Since I was the only medical assistant at that time, and it was only the doctor and office manager—who didn't offer any type of training program—I had to ask a lot of questions. The doctor was always patient about helping me, but I failed to take notes. I thought I would remember what he told me and, unfortunately, I found out that was not the case. There was so much to learn, and there was no room for error when it came to patient care.

One day I had to set up for a procedure. The doctor had shown me how to do it the day before, but I couldn't remember what number of blade to set out or what injectable to load for this certain procedure. I couldn't finish setting it up and had to ask for his help. I could tell he wasn't happy that I didn't remember what to do. I'd caused a delay in the schedule because I didn't have the sterile tray set up for him.

At the end of the day, we had a talk.

"Tina, what can you do so you don't forget what I'm teaching you?" he asked.

"From now on," I said, "I'll write down all the instructions as you're teaching me. If I have any questions, I'll ask you to review what I wrote to make sure it was correct."

He liked that approach, and that was the beginning of developing some sort of training program for the practice. I trained future staff members this way until it dawned on me to write a protocol manual that included all of the instructions. All new employees would have the information, and they could take notes as needed. To this day, I give all new employees a notebook where they can write things down that they need to remember.

4. They do the job well: Learn all aspects of your job and understand how what you do affects the business as a whole. Do your job exceptionally well every single day. Your employers will notice if you slack off after you learn your job tasks or if you delegate them to other staff members.

I established a system we use for almost every task that a staff person does. Each staff member has a list of job tasks they're assigned for their job position. As they complete most of the job tasks, they initial their work. This way, if there are any questions, we know who to ask about the task. They either initial what they've done, or a certain task is assigned to their job position.

Not long ago, this system pinpointed an employee who wasn't doing her job according to our office protocols. I'd noticed that she wasn't doing some of the job tasks that assigned to her. Others weren't being completed on time or they were half done—but she signed off on them as if they were completed. She's a great employee, and I knew that she was having some difficulties in life, but if you expect to be paid for a full day's work when you only complete 75 percent of the job, that is not okay on my watch.

At our morning huddle I decided to have a pep talk with everyone as I normally do every so often. This time my topic was "Your signature is on your work." I asked everyone if they understood that they were being paid to do the tasks they've been assigned. They all agreed that this was the case, and they also agreed that they wouldn't want to pay someone in full if that person had only done the job part way.

"Do you realize that your individual signature is on everything you do at work, every day?"

"What do you mean?" one asked.

"How many things do you do that you either sign when it's complete or are specifically assigned to do?"

They began to name all of the things where they put their signature or initials each day.

"That means you own that work. Your signature represents the effort you put into that task. When it's done correctly, it speaks volumes about what a great employee you are. In the same way, if the work is half done or not done at all, that speaks volumes about your work ethic—and not in a positive way."

I was pretty surprised that a few people hadn't realized the power of their signature.

"Your signature is like when an artist signs their work. It shows that you've put time, effort, and passion into the job and are proud of the end result."

It was a great discussion, and it solved the issue with the staff member who was having some problems.

Take pride in your work, and your employer will be proud to have you as their manager. Work with the same enthusiasm every day as you did on your first day. Always strive to do your best.

As the manager, you're the example that others will follow. If your staff sees that you're dedicated and that you work hard each day, they'll want to follow you. Be proud to put your signature on your work.

5. **They are organized:** Keep your work area clean and uncluttered. If allowed, develop a system that works for you, so you can work efficiently. You'll want to be able to retrieve all pertinent paperwork and files right away when requested or needed.

Employers don't like a messy work area because there's a higher chance that work can be misplaced or lost when you're unorganized. When your workplace is uncluttered and organized, it frees up your mind to work more productively, which is what your employer wants and what they're paying you to do. Set up systems to keep track of your daily work and that of those who report to you.

> Employers don't like a messy work area because
> there's a higher chance that work can be misplaced
> or lost when you're unorganized.

Let me tell you about someone who learned this the hard way. Dr. Minder had no idea that his manager's messy desk was a reflection of how she handled his practice financially until it was almost too late. I received an urgent call from him.

"Can you come evaluate my practice? It seems that we've cut an artery and are bleeding out financially."

He had no idea what was going on but thought it was due to not seeing enough patients. I sent a list of items and reports that I'd need to see, so I could begin my evaluation and audit. Dr. Minder said that his office manager would get the information for me.

When I arrived and asked for the items, his manager seemed a bit nervous.

"It's going to take me several weeks to get this all together," she said. She could only produce a few of the reports for me to begin my work.

This didn't make sense. I hadn't asked for anything unusual or anything that couldn't be gathered in a couple of hours, and she'd had several days to produce it. I told Dr. Minder about my concern.

"That's no surprise," he said. "Let's go to her office."

I was shocked at all of the paperwork, files, boxes, and junk that were stacked in her office. There was no clear workspace. Dr. Minder had a sick suspicion that whatever I needed was in that office somewhere—at least he hoped so.

Things got worse. When he directly asked his office manager to get a couple of things I needed, she simply didn't know where they were or if she even had them. She hadn't balanced the checking account in months, nor had she kept up on dispersing the bills to the proper accounts. We discovered that the billing was behind several weeks.

After Dr. Minder let his manager go, it took months of work for us figure everything out.

But there was a happy ending. When we got everything in order, Dr. Minder was in better shape than he thought. He hired a new, experienced manager, and together we wrote the protocols for her to follow along with a procedures manual, which he'd never done before.

One of the first things Dr. Minder asked potential manager candidates about was their organization skills. He had them submit to him how they'd set up their office drawers and desk if they were hired. He made sure that everything that had to do with running the office as far as paperwork and financial forms had a place and that he knew where that place was. He and his new manager also set up a weekly checklist of those items that showed she'd completed them. This checklist went to Dr. Minder each week for his review and signature. Great system, Dr. Minder!

6. They respect the employer's resources: You may not think this attribute is important as a manager, but it's critically important to your employer. Whether you work for a large medical organization or a solo private practice physician, their resources are highly important to them. You should never, ever waste office supplies or medical supplies.

> You should never, ever waste office supplies or medical supplies.

If you take the view that the business is yours, you'll begin see things quite differently. How would you feel if you were paying the bills for pens and coffee and toilet paper? You'd find that every paperclip has value. Be an example for your staff. Value what your employer values—which is every dollar—and you'll have greater value to your employer. Not only will you be more valuable to your employer, you'll feel good about taking care of the business overall.

So now I need to tell on myself. One day when I was at my home, I opened my dresser drawer, and as I gazed inside I saw there were about thirty pens from the office in that drawer, along with a few sticky pads, a jump drive, and some colored clips. If I came home with things like this in my scrub pockets, I wondered if other staff members also took things home without thinking about it.

The next day I told everyone at our morning huddle what I'd found in my drawer.

"Does anyone else accidentally take things home in your pockets?" I asked. I them to check and let me know the next day.

"No one's in trouble. I just realized that I did this and wanted to know if anyone else did it too?"

The next day, every single staff member brought in a variety of things that had innocently found their way to their home. It was a great opportunity to talk about costs of running the practice and how we could all help with the overall expenses. We then decided that we'd all check our pockets before we left each night.

Our doctor was very pleased to hear about this. It increased his trust that we were all going to be more aware of any waste in terms of office items because we wanted to help the practice financially.

7. They offer solutions: Employers appreciate it when managers offer solutions. They like it when you want to address problems and when you see things that can be done better. Far too often, the doctors only hear the complaints with no solutions offered.

If you have a solution to a problem or issue, the best way to approach your employer is to put it in writing. Explain what you see, what you think might be a possible solution, and why you feel that way. Ask for a time to talk to your employer to present your solution.

A manager who actively looks for ways to make the business run better and more efficiently, to raise revenue, and to increase customer satisfaction is an employer's dream employee.

> If you have a solution to a problem or issue,
> the best way to approach your employer is
> to put it in writing.

If you want to be a great manager, find solutions to improve your workplace and care about your employer's bottom line.

When I first started with our practice twenty-four years ago, I could see that there were many problems that needed to be fixed. It took a few months for me to feel comfortable enough to ask the doctor if I could make a few suggestions about what I thought were better ways to do some things in the practice. He was open to my suggestions, and although he didn't use every one of them, we collaborated on what would be the best way to take care of certain situations or problems.

Now I realize that I don't have the answers for all of our practice issues, even though my staff may think I should. I depend on each person in our practice to give their input regarding procedures, protocols, and systems, in order to be the most efficient.

Invite your staff members to submit a complaint or problem they're having along with their solution to fix it. Using this approach, we've fixed lots of problems by working together to solve issues. When people are a part of the solution, they're more likely to adhere to that solution than they would be if someone else came up with a fix for everyone to follow.

Chapter 3

Practices of Great Communicators

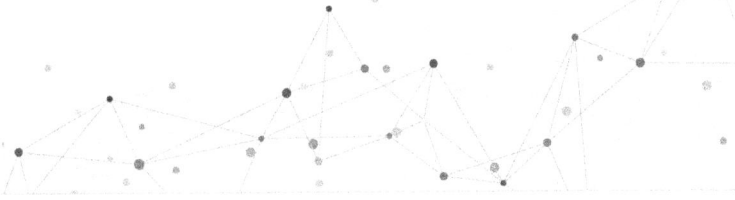

The problem with communication . . .
is the illusion that is has been accomplished.
~George Benard Shaw

WHAT MAKES A GREAT MANAGER? It's someone who's learned good communications skills and takes the time to use them. Many great leaders displayed excellent communication skills. Abraham Lincoln, Winston Churchill, Billy Graham, and Gandhi are just a few on the list.

All great communicators possess the following attributes; these are what draw people to them:

- They're trustworthy and sincere.
- They're specific in their communications.
- They focus on the listener.
- They have an open mind and open communications.

You can learn these skills and develop them even further. Practice is necessary to develop any good skill, and communication skills are necessary for success—not only in the workplace, but in all of your life.

Let's take a look at these attributes and how they play into daily communication in the workplace.

Trust and Sincerity

Would you take advice from or follow someone that you didn't trust? Of course not. Yet in the workplace there are often times you have to trust your supervisors because of their position. Later you might find out that they failed to be trustworthy, as in the example below.

Bill and Mary worked in the same department in a large medical organization that had several doctors and departments. Because Bill was a manager, he had access to executive information about organizational issues that Mary didn't have.

Mary was concerned because there'd been times when Bill had given her information about upcoming changes in company policies, future business ventures, and departmental issues that proved to be false when the information was disseminated throughout the corporation.

She oversaw one of the medical practices in the organization and was in charge of scheduling staff, managing supplies for the department, and leading team huddles each morning. It was her job to keep the staff updated on their individual doctor's practice department and to announce any upcoming changes in the organization that would directly affect their department.

Mary needed to rely on Bill to give her the facts; he'd told her organizational gossip that he said were facts, and she'd passed that information on to the staff. When the information was proved incorrect, it made her look incompetent. She was afraid that if she trusted what Bill said, it might affect her job.

Bill, however, liked the fact that his position was above Mary and a few other practice managers. He felt like his job was more important, and he wanted Mary and the other managers to see him in that light. So, he told them bits information he might know, some of which was hearsay, to make himself feel more important than they were.

This can happen in small medical practices, too, when the office manager—because they know more about the overall practice due to their close communication with the physician, accountants, and other professionals—spreads gossip. They tell bits and pieces of what the doctor may be thinking without telling the whole story. It makes them feel important to get privileged information from the doctor that the staff doesn't have access to. It's an ugly power issue, and it doesn't foster a great work environment or a cohesive team. Office managers are not above the rest of the staff members; they are part of the team with their own job tasks.

If you're the office manager, communicate only the facts about the practice and what the doctor has authorized you to share. If you add some unnecessary fluff or hearsay, you're undermining the organization. You won't be trusted by the staff, which will cost the practice because you'll be the reason that they leave.

> If you're the office manager, communicate only the facts about the practice and what the doctor has authorized you to share.

There's a very simple rule to apply: simply tell the truth and only when you are authorized to tell it. Sometimes managers think it's a good idea to hold back from telling the *whole* truth. Maybe they think it will give them a power card at some point, or maybe it makes them feel important to know something that others don't. If you do this, you'll hinder productivity and destroy work relationships. No company can afford this.

If others depend on you for important information, here are three key steps to follow to make sure you're not leading them astray:

1. Just the facts: Speak the facts as they were presented to you. The facts—and only the facts—matter. Only share them when you have permission to do so.
2. No opinions: Don't add your opinion or interpretation of what you think or "feel" was said. Otherwise, you'll shade the original truth.
3. Core communication: Make sure you know what the original communicator said *and what it means to them*. If you didn't quite understand the message, ask them to explain what they meant, so you don't pass on information that could be misinterpreted.

Not only do others depend on your communications to be accurate, but your reputation depends on it as well. If you share false or inaccurate information, you can damage your own career.

Be the bearer of fact-based communications only. Your co-workers will appreciate working with someone that they can rely on and trust.

Be Specific

There's so much opportunity for misunderstanding in communications and, as the manager, it's your job to be specific about what you communicate. The problem occurs when you think you've been specific, but your staff members don't actually understand what you said.

This came to light for me at a recent conference where the keynote speaker's topic was communication. David Frees was enlightening and his message was thought provoking. He asked the audience to participate in the most eye-opening demonstration of communication principles I've ever seen.

> The problem occurs when you think you've been specific, but your staff members don't actually understand what you said.

The audience broke up into groups of six. Each group had to pick one of two topics: either *sex* or *learning*. Then we chose a spokesperson for our team. It was a contest between teams.

After we selected our topic, which was sex, each person had to write down ten words that described the topic. When we finished, the spokesperson read each person's list aloud to the group. If everyone in the group had written the same word on their list, our group would get one point. In fact, we'd get one point for each word that made it on all of our lists.

Out of twenty groups, only a few of the groups earned a single point. Even though each person was writing about same topic—either sex or learning—they all picked different words to describe it.

Our group got zero points. In fact, only twice did anyone have even one of the same words I'd written down. Even though we were all thinking about the same topic, we didn't think about it the same way.

This happens all the time. Communication is very difficult. If you ask a team member to do something, they could be thinking of something totally different from what you meant to convey. When you talk to others and are trying to get a point across, ask them to repeat what they heard to be sure you're on the same page.

So, what can you do to make yourself understood?

Let's take what happened in the situation above and apply it to your workplace. If you want to gather information from a coworker, take the time to develop questions that will invite them to give the information you need. Let's say you need to find a form the doctor needs to sign for a patient.

You ask, "Do you remember Ms. Jones?"

"Yes."

"Didn't she want the doctor to sign her physical therapy orders?"

"Yes."

"Did he agree to do that?"

"I think so."

"Did he sign the order?"

"Yes."

"Do you know where it is?"

What a long, drawn out way to ask a simple question: "Do you know if Ms. Jones's physical therapy order was signed by the doctor yet?" Too many times we add so much extra garbage to our questions when we could simply be direct. This is distracting and aggravating and can ultimately lead to getting the wrong answer—and in the medical field it could become a liability issue.

> Too many times we add so much extra garbage to our questions when we could simply be direct.

Below are three great questions you can use to cut out the extra fluff and get directly to the point. By asking these questions, you save time and your communication is more specific and direct.

1. If you have a question that isn't vital at that moment ask, **"I have a question. Is this a good time for you?"** This gives the other person the freedom to either say yes or to let you know when they can help you without interrupting their workflow. That way, they can speak to you and focus on what you're saying. If you're considerate of their time, they will also be of yours.

2. When a co-worker comes to you with a problem or issue, your first question should be, **"What are the facts, so I can fully understand this issue?"** This one simple question can save a ton of time. It's important to get all of the facts when trying to resolve a problem, and all parties involved will appreciate it. Keep it short, simple, and specific. Just the facts please!

3. This last question is one that we use frequently in our medical practice. If somebody asks this question, you must respond immediately if at all possible. Here's the question: **"I need your help, can you please (fill in the blank)"** This couldn't be more clear. You're directly asking someone for help and you let them know exactly what they can do for you.

When you ask clear questions, not only can you get things done, but you save time by using communication techniques that are specific and direct.

Focus on the Listener

If you ask why someone thinks their manager is amazing, most often they'll tell you it's because that manager listens to them. It's essential to listen to your staff, and honing your listening skills is an ongoing process. It's not always easy to take the time to listen to someone, especially when you're at work. You have so many things you're already thinking about, and it's hard to stop what you're doing and change your focus. You have to shift your thoughts to try to understand what the person is saying. That's not an easy task.

No matter what your position, good listening skills are essential in the workplace. But as a manager, your people expect you to listen to them. And the patients expect you to listen to their problems or desires, so you can help them.

Hearing what people say is one thing; listening is another. Hearing means you take in the speaker's message, but it doesn't necessarily mean the message was received, processed, or responded to. Listening means you received the message, processed what was said to make sense of it, then responded in a way that shows understanding of what was said.

> Hearing what people say is one thing; listening is another.

According to Dick Lee and Delmar Hatesohl of the University of Missouri Extension, most people use only 25 percent to 30 percent of their listening potential. And we speak at a rate of 125 to150 words per minute—but we can listen and receive about 400 to 500 words per minute. It's easy to see how you can lose interest in what someone's saying and stop paying attention. You get distracted because they're speaking slower than you can listen. That's why we often don't really hear what someone else is saying. Your mind is light-years ahead of their words.

Here are some things you can do to focus on what another person is saying:

- Face the person who's speaking to you. Focus on the words they're saying. It's okay to ask them to repeat what they said; at least they'll know you're trying to understand them.

- Keep quiet until they have finished what they have to say. Don't jump to conclusions and don't start talking before they are finished.

- Take a moment to process what was said and what your response should be before you answer. Then answer them directly or ask a question for clarification.

When someone takes the time to really listen to you, you feel respected, cared for, satisfied, and understood. It's a positive experience that fosters better relationships, better quality of work, greater cooperation, and less stress.

I believe that good listening skills are the most important skills to have, not only as a manager, but in life. Did you catch that part above about how listening creates better relationships? Relationships are important in every area of life. People need to know that you care about them, and when you listen to them, it shows that you do.

Open Mind, Open Communication

Employers, supervisors, and managers often communicate very casually with their staff members, like they would their friends. But at work, your coworkers and staff may need a more structured style of communication. Everyone in the office works together to make the organization more profitable and successful. Managers need to know how to most effectively communicate with their staff, so everyone knows what's expected of them.

So, how can you make your communication clearer? Open communication starts when the employee is hired. You should explain their job tasks and how they will be trained to do them. Be clear about what you expect them to accomplish and how instructions will be given to them. Explain the communication policy, and tell them the process for getting their questions answered and their problems solved. Discuss how you'll approach them if a mistake is made, and how you typically handle such a situation. Any consequences for errors should be outlined in detail, verbally and in writing.

Problems will invariably arise if you don't know how to effectively communicate with the people who work for and with you. If you let them know what to expect up front and how the policies are handled, these chances are minimized. It's like preventative maintenance on your car. You don't wait until it breaks down; you take care of it beforehand to avoid problems.

Open communication is when expressing ideas and objections in a free exchange is encouraged between everyone—staff, managers, and employers. To get to that place, start with these baby steps.

1. Take time to communicate. Everyone is so rushed these days and has so much to accomplish at work and home. Take those extra few minutes to ask everyone you work with how their day's going and what's going on at home. Do it every day. It's important to get a little personal with

your staff, within the boundaries of each person's comfort zone. It shows that you care about your coworkers outside of work and creates bonds between workmates.

2. Listen, listen, listen! Actively listen. Ask questions, and listen between the lines to discover what's really being said. Be quiet and try to understand your coworker's point of view. Don't assume you know what he or she said. Ask for clarification, so you know that you understand what they meant.

3. If you're the manager or business owner, enlist ideas from your staff members that could help run your business better. These are your frontline people who deal with your patients every day. Because they talk to your patients, they know what these customers want. Take time to listen to your staff and then implement their ideas when possible. It will not only help your business, but it will let that person know that you value them and their input.

4. When you listen to your staff and take action on their ideas, you show that you don't want a communication hierarchy. Instead, you encourage open communication with everyone who works there. After you do this a few times, the staff will be more open to offering their thoughts and talking to you about issues that concern them. That's what you want. Remember that you're working together toward common goals that will make the practice grow.

5. Finally, take the time to celebrate together, whether it's because the business saw more new customers this month than last, or just because it's Friday. Enjoy each other's company as co-workers and friends. You probably spend more time at work each week than you do at home, so it's worth it to develop good relationships with your co-workers.

An open, communicative environment makes the workplace better. Creating an environment where everyone is growing and engaged with each other is healthy. Your people should be happy to come to work every day. Life is too short to work in an unpleasant environment.

Chapter 4

Be The Manager They Need

Do right. Do your best.
Treat others as you want to be treated.
~ Lou Holtz

SEVERAL YEARS AGO, I was consulting with a medical practice. The physician told me he was bothered by one of his newer medical assistant's behavior.

"What's the problem?" I asked.

"She doesn't seem to be dedicated to the practice," he answered. "Since her first day, I've watched her as it gets close to 5:00 p.m. She starts cleaning up her desk and getting everything ready for the next day around 4:50. Then when the clock strikes five, she runs out the door. And every morning she arrives right as the clock strikes eight."

"Is she supposed to stay past five?" I asked.

"Not technically," he said. "But no one else is rushing out the door at five. Sometimes they're still on the phone, or a patient might still be here and they wait."

"Have you talked to the employee about this?" I asked.

"I had my manager talk to her. Stacey asked the new gal why she always left at five, and all she got back was another question: 'Aren't our hours eight to five?' she said. We didn't take it any further than that, but it still bugs me. I don't know if I should keep her. She does the job fine, but she doesn't seem very loyal to the practice."

I visited this practice for several days and got to speak with each of the staff members. I asked this particular employee about her professional goals and desires. She was very nice, had a great attitude, and said that she loved her job and helping all the patients. She wished she had time to further her education in the medical profession, so she could be of more help, but at this time in her life, that wasn't possible.

"Why not?" I asked.

"I don't have time," she said. "I'm a single mom of three boys. They all go to different schools, and they all play soccer. I rush home every day to pick them up and then have to get them to different locations for practice."

Ah! So that's why she left right at five. "What are your mornings like?" I asked.

"They're even more stressful," she said. "I have to track every minute to get them to their three separate schools and then get to work on time. I haven't been late yet, but I'm always worried that I will be. I'm so thankful for this job and want to do a great job for the doctor. He's such a good person and physician."

Wow! The doctor had certainly pegged this one wrong. His idea of what was going on was completely different from what was really happening.

It's easy to make incorrect judgements if you trust your first impressions of people and situations. Misjudging others is a topic that should be openly discussed. It's important to hold yourself accountable to find out the facts before you pass judgment. Ask what's going on. Communicate if you have questions. Avoid harboring resentments that come from assuming you know what's going on—when you really don't.

Judgment by First Impressions

First impressions are formed in the first five to seven seconds of seeing someone. Seems ridiculous, doesn't it? Who can know what someone's really like or what the situation involves in just a few seconds?

Sadly, we draw such conclusions all the time. You see someone, and based on what you see, you make a judgment about that person: what they're like, whether they're nice or not, what's going on with them. Too often, that first impression is your final impression. And the first impression usually comes from what you *see*.

I read an interesting story a while back that explained how we think with our eyes first. In Harry Beckwith and Christine Clifford's book, *You Inc.*, they presented this topic in a chapter called "People Buy You with Their Eyes." They state that "people think with their eyes" and "people hear what they see."

They go on to tell a story about a thirty-second bank commercial that verbally stated *three times* that the bank had better information that customers need to make better financial decisions. To illustrate the point, they showed a mountain climber who was preparing to climb. He was studying maps and weather charts before making his ascent.

The viewers of the commercial never heard the "better information" words spoken at all, even though the commercial repeated that message three times. When asked about the message of the commercial, the viewers thought that the bank was communicating that they—the bank— were *strong*.

The producers were stunned. How did the viewers get that idea? Easy: they saw a man carefully preparing for a climbing trip. And then an image of the man rock climbing flashed on the screen for less than four seconds. The visual message of his strength overwhelmed the verbal message of his prior planning.

As you go through your day, notice how much you think with your eyes. I think you'll be amazed. The more you keep this exercise top-of-mind, the better you can determine what's really in front of you. Too often we make snap judgments about other people, which can be detrimental to relationships at work.

Allowing Outside Influences To Color Your Impressions

Before you form an impression about someone else, be sure it's based on what you personally know as fact. Although it's important to listen to what others say about another person, it's also important to come to your own conclusions about who that person really is. It's not easy to do, particularly after you've heard a negative opinion about him or her. Don't base your impressions on hearsay. People's true colors eventually shine through, whether they're good or bad.

I recently had a conversation with an office manager who was having a hard time choosing the right candidate for a job opening. She said she'd narrowed it down to two people, but she couldn't decide which one to select.

"What's the struggle?" I asked.

"One candidate had most of the skill qualifications," she said. "I liked her during the interview, but she didn't have any experience, which is a detriment. She'll need extensive training, and that will take a lot of time."

"What about the other candidate?" I asked.

"She has everything I'm looking for. She did well during the interview, I liked her personality, and she had the experience we need. She could hit the floor running with very little training. But there's one thing that makes me wonder if she'd be a good employee.

"One of my staff members already knew her. They went to school together. But she told me this candidate had some really bad habits and got in trouble when they were in high school. So, I'm apprehensive about hiring her."

"How long ago was that?" I asked.

"Oh, that was over ten years ago. She doesn't know the woman now. She just remembers what she was like in high school."

Clearly, this manager let what her staff member said color her own impression of this person, who was the best qualified candidate for the job. In fact, she didn't offer her the job because of what she'd heard.

This made me wonder what people I knew back in high school would think of me. Did they think I was still the same now as I was when I was a teenager? Did my adolescent behavior color their opinion of who I am now?

Our impressions of people and their impression of us can stick, sometimes for a lifetime. It's wise to consider how important impressions are.

Every Encounter Makes an Impression

One of my job tasks is to take the deposits to the bank. It always seems time consuming, when I feel my time could be better spent at the office. For preventing embezzlement, it's a smart business practice to have one person prepare the deposit and have someone else take it to the bank. So, the job is mine.

To make it interesting, I've taken up the hobby of people-watching and listening to surrounding conversations while I'm waiting in line for a teller. I've heard and witnessed several engaging things at the bank, and now I actually look forward to my weekly visits to see what I might learn.

A recent incident made an impression on me. When it was his turn, the gentleman in front of me gave the teller the check he was depositing. She looked at it and said she knew the man who'd written it. He was her son's coach.

"Really?" he said. "I work for him."

"Lucky you," she said. "It must be wonderful to work for such a nice person."

"It is," he said, and then he told her about a few of the nice things his employer does in the community in addition to coaching children's sports.

"Well, my son really loves him as a coach and doesn't want to play for anyone else. In fact, all of the parents have high respect for him and how he handles our kids."

As she closed out the transaction, she said, "Goodbye. When you see Wayne, please tell him I said hello."

This conversation took place in the matter of a few minutes, but it started me thinking.

If one of my staff members met someone that I knew in a similar situation, what would they say about me? Would they speak as highly of me as this man and the teller had about the man they both knew? Would their opinion be different from what I think it should be?

Your reputation speaks loudly about who you are, and it can make or break you as a manager. It's a good practice to evaluate yourself as a manager—to write up a report card on yourself and to seek out good, honest feedback about how others view you. I've done this in a few ways.

One way is that I have two people I go to and bounce off my ideas, problems, and solutions. My Aunt Dollie is my number one mentor, and she's always been willing to listen and give suggestions. My people skills and management skills would not be at their current level without her advice. Everyone needs at least one great mentor, and I've been blessed to have a couple of them. It's good to have a sounding board.

Another way I evaluate myself, although it can be a little painful, is to ask the people I work with some honest questions about my management skills. Am I a good leader and role model? What can I improve or do to become a better manager?

I've been amazed at some things I learned that I was unaware of, like how they watched me when I was upset and had to handle tough situations, or how I showed that I cared for them in times when I didn't realize how much my actions meant to them. There was also some tough input, like how one person thought that I favored another staff member. I didn't realize that my actions gave this impression, but to this person, they did. You can become a better person through evaluating—and then improving—the areas where you have shortcomings.

Take a look at the questions that follow and answer them honestly. Self-evaluations aren't easy, but this exercise will help you better understand where you are now as a manager and what you can change to become the kind of manager that the staff love to work with and the physicians want to run their practice.

Office Manager Self Evaluation

Name:

Date:

Physician(s):

Length of Time in Management Position:
1. **Vision:** Has a compelling vision for my office or department and where it should be in one year; in five years. Has a "big picture" perspective that identifies opportunities and threats for the medical practice. Understands how my position and responsibilities fit into the company/ physician's vision.
   Score (1-10):
   Comments:

   _____

   _____

   _____

   _____

   _____

2. **Communication:** Ability to communicate the vision and inspire others to buy into it. Communicates well with the practice physician(s) and all staff members. Supports the overall practice vision and my role in it.
   Score (1-10):

Comments:

_____

_____

_____

_____

_____

3. **Goals**: Clearly articulates the goals and responsibilities that will move the practice toward the vision the physicians have stated. Has personal goals for growth as a manager in education and office production. Helps staff to form personal goals and team office goals.
   Score (1-10):

   Comments:

_____

_____

_____

_____

_____

4. **Focus/Delegation/Management Skills**: Maintains focused attention on the critical areas or projects that require a manger's leadership. Effectively delegates to other staff members to accomplish the needs of the office on a daily basis. Continually grows in personal management skills, i.e., education, books, seminars, classes, etc. Has

a good understanding of podiatry and keeps current in changes and updates in the podiatric community.

Score (1-10):

Comments:

_____

_____

_____

_____

_____

5. **Passion/Commitment:** Is enthusiastic and dedicated to the practice, its physicians, and staff members as a whole. Is passionate and committed to my position of office manager.

   Score (1-10):

   Comments:

   _____

   _____

   _____

   _____

   _____

   _____

6. **People:** Can attract and keep great people. Puts the right people in the right positions. Recruits, trains, and retains a top-quality staff that works together as a team.

Committed to helping staff members grow. Invests in the staff to help them achieve their highest potential and builds star employees who really shine. Am I a *star builder?* Always builds them up to make them successful.

Score (1-10):

Comments:

_____

_____

_____

_____

_____

_____

7. **"Star Builder":** Develops career development plans for each staff member.

Score (1-10):

Comments:

_____

_____

_____

_____

_____

_____

8. **Connected:** Is connected to my office team. Knows their goals, strengths, and weaknesses. Has meaningful

interaction every day with each person on the office team. My office team thinks of me first when they have a question or idea they want to express.

Score (1-10):

Comments:

_____

_____

_____

_____

_____

_____

9. **Availability**: Is readily available to the staff in the office. Maintains regular "office hours." If I'm out of the office, the staff knows when I will return and how to reach me. Manages by walking around. I'm aware of what's going on in the office at all times.

Score: (1-10):

Comments:

_____

_____

_____

_____

_____

_____

10. **Facilities:** Maintains the office in a neat, orderly fashion that inspires confidence that we are organized and in control. Office facilities are neat, clean, freshly painted, and updated to inspire an environment of success. Paper and supplies are organized and easily available. The office environment is easy to conduct business in.

Score (1-10):

Comment:

_____

_____

_____

_____

_____

_____

11. **Control/Responsibilities**: Takes control and responsibility for the office within my boundaries. Knows when to ask others for advice or help, but never expects others to do my job. Knows how to make decisions and how to stay connected with my physicians and the office support staff. Supports the concept of "the team that works hard together stays together."

Score (1-10):

Comments:

_____

_____

_____

_____

_____

_____

12. **Systems**: Creates, operates, and maintains systems that add value and make it easier for patients and other physician offices to conduct business with our practice.
Score (1-10):
Comments:

_____

_____

_____

_____

_____

_____

13. **Patient Service Rating:** Establishes systems, training, and measurements to have a patient-friendly environment that delivers world-class service. Communicates the importance of patient satisfaction to entire team. Handles patient issues in positive ways, improving relationships and building strong foundations with them.
Score (1-10):

Comments:

_____

_____

_____

_____

_____

14. **Knowledge/Competence/Learning:** Has the knowledge base to be effective in the position. Knows how to do all other staff positions. Is continuously seeking new knowledge and ways to improve and make the practice better. Creates a "learning environment" in the office. Has understanding of state and federal law in handling employee issues. Accurate knowledge of OSHA and Medicare compliance rules.
    Score (1-10)
    Comments:

_____

_____

_____

_____

_____

_____

15. **Business Generator**: Continuously looks for new ways to bring patients to the practice. Understands

the importance of physician and other outside referral sources. Understands the products that are dispensed in the office. Establishes relationships with product vendors.
Score (1-10):
Comments:

_____

_____

_____

_____

_____

_____

16. **Change**: Anticipates and leads change.
Score (1-10):
Comments:

_____

_____

_____

_____

_____

_____

17. **Trust:** Is trusted to treat people fairly and keep confidences. Has credibility. Is reliable and can be relied on to do what is promised and required.
Score (1-10):

Comments:

_____

_____

_____

_____

_____

_____

18. **Decision Making**: Makes good decisions. Has a system for gathering input and making decisions that is consistent and well understood by the physician(s) and staff.
Score (1-10):
Comments:

_____

_____

_____

_____

_____

_____

19. **Positive Attitude/Encourager**: Creates a positive environment that encourages others to succeed.
Score (1-10):

Comments:

_____

_____

_____

_____

20. **Strengths:** What specific strengths do you have as a manager? How could these strengths be leveraged for greater positive impact within the practice?

_____

_____

_____

_____

_____

21. **Weaknesses:** What specific areas of improvement would help you to be a more effective manager?

_____

_____

_____

_____

_____

_____

Appearance/Influences/Impressions

I had the wonderful opportunity a few years ago to speak to a group of medical office managers and assistants in Ontario, Canada. It was refreshing because they were interested in learning how they could be better employees and how they could make their workplace better for themselves and their coworkers.

It was a full-day workshop, and we discussed five different topics. One topic was "The Power of Presentation," where I addressed the power of first impressions. Each time I've presented this topic, I'm reminded of how we form impressions in the blink of an eye.

It is really true that, "You never get a second chance to make a first impression." First impressions usually stick and are rarely changed. When you're at work, you're an ambassador for the practice and the physician owner(s). The impression you give not only reflects on you, but directly on the physician business owner(s).

> First impressions usually stick and are
> rarely changed.

If an employee is dressed sloppily, inappropriately, or is wearing a soiled uniform, what kind of impression do they make? Patients will not only think poorly of the employee, they'll wonder about the competence of the physician who allows an employee to come to work in such a state. Some employees think it's unfair that their appearance carries such weight, but the fact is that it does.

Look at the Disney Properties; all the employees are clean and neat from Snow White to the sanitation workers. You'll never see wrinkled clothing on any of them. That's the way Walt Disney wanted it, and that's the way it's remained. He knew that appearances carry a lot of weight and influenced how people viewed his business.

When I closed my presentation, I asked the group a question: If appearances don't mean that much, then why do people spend millions upon millions of dollars on brands like Prada, Dior, and Gucci?

It only takes an extra minute to look at yourself in the mirror before you step out the door to ask yourself, "What type of impression will I give today when someone sees me?"

Isn't the impression you give at work worth it?

Chapter 5

Create an "A" Team

Unity is strength. When there is teamwork and collaboration, wonderful things can be achieved.
~ Mattie Stepanek

I WAS ALWAYS IN A HURRY to fill an open position, so the practice would continue to run well. But many times, I didn't complete all of the hiring steps that I do now. Needless to say, this led to some problems. Such was the case when I hired Paradise, (not her real name) to be the front office receptionist.

We'd previously hired a great person to run our front office, and after thirty days, we had our first review together. I was really happy with her and was ready to give her a bit of a raise and move forward with her training when she dropped a bomb.

"I've decided that I don't like feet, and I'm giving you my two-week notice."

What! I didn't see this coming at all. But, I couldn't make her stay, and she agreed to help train the new hire if I could find someone right away.

I immediately published an ad, and the next day I received a few resumes. What luck! One candidate had worked for a physician that my doctor was acquainted with. My doctor called that physician and asked his wife, who ran the practice, about the candidate.

"She only worked for us for a few months. She didn't catch on very fast, but she was a friendly and happy person. We let her go because we no longer needed extra help."

I bet they didn't have a training program like we do, so she'll probably learn much faster working with my team, I thought.

I called Paradise, and sure enough, she was a very happy person. She had what I call a sparkly personality. She agreed to come in right away to talk with the doctor, our lead team member, and me. She park her bicycle in front of the office. Her appearance was nice—a little retro in attire and a sixties hairstyle. She was cute.

She answered our questions appropriately and was funny in a quirky way. I should have paid attention when a red flag was raised when she reached in her bag and pulled out a giant seashell. She told us a little story about it and said she was taking it to her mother after she left the office. Instead of heeding that red flag, we offered her the job without interviewing anyone else. We only had eight days for our current receptionist to train her.

It only took four days to realize that Paradise lived in paradise, and it was true that she didn't catch on to even the simplest of tasks. During a training session with my lead team member, she wrapped scotch tape around her wrist and arm instead of taking notes. I knew she had to go.

It was my fault for hiring her in a rush without giving her any task tests that I normally do. If I'd only done that, I would have realized that she couldn't pay attention or follow directions.

"You can't fire me," she said. "I turned in my bike and bought a car. I have payments to make!"

Of course, I felt terrible about that, but we certainly couldn't let her stay. At that point, I promised myself and the practice that I'd never again make a hasty hire.

I've been an office manager over two decades now, and I've had to hire and fire more staff than I've wanted. It's part of being in business. I know that since I work with people, I'll have people problems.

But some of those problems were of my own making because I chose the wrong person for the job and took too long to let them go. I thought it would get easier to find the right employees now that I'm a more seasoned manager. But it still takes time—and a lot of it.

I don't know anyone who likes searching for new employees. We all want to hire great people to enhance our team, but trying to find the right person is a daunting task, although it's always time well spent. Your goal is to find the perfect fit, which means that the person has to work well with you and your team. And that person must be excited about their new job.

A colleague of mine, Jay Henderson (the owner of Real Talent Hiring), is an expert in the finding and hiring the right person for the job. In his book, *The Ultimate Small Business Guide to Hiring Super-Stars*, he says that when posting a job ad, it's okay to create a hoop or two for the applicants to jump through.

For example, when writing the ad, instruct the applicant to reply with the subject line, "I am the best person for your team." If they don't put that in the subject line, don't consider them. Since they didn't follow this simple direction, they probably won't follow your instructions after they're hired. Jay has other insightful tips that make hiring easier, and I highly recommend his book.

The Foundation

When coaching other medical offices, I'm often asked questions like these: How do I know who's the right person to hire? How much do I pay them? How do I train them? How can I make them want to stay?

When you build a house, you start with the foundation—the most essential part of the building. Failure to install an appropriate foundation leads to certain disaster. The same is true for your office. You need to construct a good foundation on which you can build your office staff. That means you have systems in place when you bring in new staff members, and you properly train them to become a valuable member of your team.

> You need to construct a good foundation on which you can build your office staff.

First, how do you hire the right person for the job? Start by reading Jay's book as recommended. Hiring isn't an easy task, but you can make the process easier by becoming a better interviewer. Prepare for your interviews. Before you meet your applicants, spend time looking over their application and resume. Are there any areas you question, such as a lapse in employment that they didn't account for?

In chapter 1, we discussed creating a job description for the office manager. You also need to create a job description for every staff position (sample job descriptions follow). Each description should contain the qualifications for the specific position.

For example, if you're hiring a front office assistant, they'll be responsible for computer input, scheduling appointments, and taking payments. So, you want to be sure that the applicant can type, spell correctly, and listen carefully to a message and transfer the correct information to paper. Computer skills and accuracy are a must for this position.

Following are sample job descriptions for a back office medical assistant and an administrative medical assistant:

POSITION OVERVIEW:
Back Office Medical Assistant

Name: **Job Title:** Back office medical assistant

Hire Date: **Revision Date:**

Primary Essential Job Function:

Prepare for patients' arrival by reviewing the schedule and anticipating what needs to be prepared in advance for each patient.

Assist doctor in the flow of patients in and out of the treatment room in an efficient way by following office protocols. Obtain all information needed from patients prior to doctor entering the treatment room. Complete intake and documentation, so the doctor can understand the patient's immediate need. Close appointment with patient when the doctor leaves room.

Assist doctor with in-office procedures. Follow office protocols and follow sterile technique with set up, assisting, and clean up.

Have full understanding of patient appointment initial scheduling and follow-up protocols.

Possess excellent knowledge and ability in regard to patient service skills, patient etiquette, and personal appearance protocols of the practice.

Have full understanding and adhere to all office protocols that pertain to the position of back office assistant per physician's approval.

Required Job Tasks for Position:
- Room patients and perform intakes
- Take patient vitals
- Answer phone and schedule appointments
- Schedule surgery
- Shoe sales and shoe fitting
- DME fitting and dispensing
- Take x-rays
- Sterile technique and instrument sterilization
- Clean, stock, and organize exam rooms
- Inventory control and order supplies
- Diabetic shoe fitting and dispensing
- Order orthotics
- Strapping and padding per physician's protocols
- Prepare and give patients whirlpool therapy
- Perform vascular exams.

Requirements:	Meets Requirements:	Requires Training:
Patient service training:		
Computer software training:		
Scheduling protocols:		
X-ray techniques and laws:		
Sterile technique:		
Shoe fitting and dispensing:		
Knowledge of whirlpool therapy		
Knowledge of proper strapping		
Knowledge of proper padding		
Performing vascular exams		
Knowledge of DME dispensing:		
Personal appearance protocols:		
Proficient in nail debridement:		
Proficient in diabetic sensory testing:		
Understands and performs office protocols of patient assistance and office flow.		
Understands and fulfills daily, weekly, and monthly tasks.		
Has received and understands Practice long-term goals.		

Position Overview:
Administrative Medical Assistant

Name: **Job Title:** Administrative medical assistant
Hire Date: **Revision Date:**

Primary Essential Job Function:

To provide excellent patient service to each patient, either in the office or over the phone. Make the patient feel comfortable and that they've called the perfect office where they can be treated.

Perform office-opening tasks in preparation for patient visits. Check and record all messages left on answering machine.

Have full understanding of what paperwork needs to be obtained and completed for each patient visit. Input new patient paperwork to computer system, have complete knowledge of insurance, medications, authorizations, and medical history obtained and input all properly into computer.

Properly prepare for patient arrival by reviewing the schedule and anticipating what needs to be done for each patient's visit to the office. Verify any balances or copayments that are due.

Update the existing patient information, insurance, and demographics in the computer, so there's no delay in patient billing or communications. Perform insurance verifications for copayments, deductibles, and benefits.

Be proficient in answering the phone and possess full knowledge on how to triage patients and place them into the daily schedule. Take accurate messages and get them to the physician or other staff member according to urgency.

Understand protocols for releasing patient medical records. Obtain proper permission signatures and release only to persons who are approved according to the HIPAA guidelines. Scan all pertinent paperwork into patient charts. Fax any information to patient's PCP or other facilities to expedite patient care.

Handle office petty cash. Record cash payments and give receipts. Count and balance daily payment sheet.

Prepares all routing slips and paperwork for billing company.

Perform reminder calls to all patients the day before their appointment; remind them of any paperwork that's needed for their appointment.

Possess excellent knowledge and ability with regard to patient service skills, patient etiquette, and personal appearance protocols of the practice.

Schedule surgery.

Have full understanding and adhere to all office protocols that pertain to the position of administrative podiatric office assistant per physician's approval.

Job Tasks Required of Position:

- Understands great patient service requirements
- Understands and can perform all office opening tasks
- Understands triage methods according to office protocols
- Full understanding of computer medical software to perform job tasks
- Understands insurance coverage information
- Understands and performs authorizations for patient benefits and visits
- Ability to take accurate phone messages and relay them
- Full understanding of the HIPAA policy and able to explain it to patients
- Understand protocols for releasing and obtaining medical records for patients and physicians
- Can handle money exchanges and balance a day sheet
- Understands schedule systems and is able to schedule patients according to protocols to ensure a full patient load, if possible. The goal is to see the maximum number of patients in the time allowed.
- Excellent typing and phone skills
- Excellent people and relational skills

Requirements:	Meets Requirements:	Requires Training:
Patient service training:		
Computer software training:		
Scheduling protocols:		
Personal appearance protocols:		
Understands and performs office protocols of patient assistance and office flow:		
Understands and fulfills daily, weekly, and monthly tasks:		
Fully understands surgery scheduling:		
Has received and understands practice's long-term goals:		
Perform insurance verifications:		
Perform insurance authorizations:		
Trained and understands HIPAA:		
Able to fill out and balance day sheet:		
Understands podiatric terminology to perform job tasks		

When you sit down to interview the applicant, make sure the atmosphere is comfortable. They're going to be nervous, and you want them to feel comfortable, so they're more willing to open up and talk to you. A comfortable conversation can reveal information that will be helpful to you in the hiring process. Depending on who is doing the interviewing in your office (the doctor or the office manager), you might open the interview by telling the applicant a little about how you got into the medical field or some history of the practice. This will put the person at ease and set you up for a comfortable conversation.

Your interview questions must always comply with your state laws. Here are few questions that are unlawful in most states. There may be some off-limits questions for which you want to know the answers, so I've provided a specific way of asking that may be helpful to you:

- Religion: You **cannot** ask about the applicant's religious denomination or affiliations.

- Marital status: You **cannot** ask whether the applicant is married or not.

- Children: You **cannot** ask if the applicant has children. You **can** tell the applicant what the working hours are and ask if they have any problems with working those hours. Many times, the applicant will reveal information about childcare, but you can't specifically ask about children and childcare unless the applicant brings it up first.

- Age: You **cannot** ask how old the applicant is, but you can ask if they are eighteen years or older.

- Disabilities: You **cannot** ask, "Do you have a disability?" But you **can** ask, "Do you have any impairments that would interfere with your ability to perform the job for which you have applied?

- Birthplace: You **cannot** ask the applicant their birthplace, or their parent's birthplace, or their wife or other close relative's birthplace.

- Citizenship: You **cannot** ask an applicant if he or she is a naturalized or native-born citizen or the date when they acquired citizenship. You **cannot** ask, "Of what country are you a citizen?" You **can** ask any of the following: Are you a citizen of the United States? If you are not a United States citizen, do you have the legal right to remain in the United States to work?

- Education: You **can** ask about the applicant's academic, vocational, or professional education and the public and private schools they attended. You **cannot** ask dates attended or graduated.

- Driver's license: You **can** ask, "Do you possess a valid driver's license?" But you **cannot** ask to see their driver's license prior to employment.

How you phrase your questions is important. You want the applicants to tell you as much as possible about themselves. With that in mind, don't ask questions that can be answered "Yes" or "No." Instead of, "Have you ever been in charge of answering the phones?" say, "Tell me about your experience with being in charge of answering the phones." This will encourage the applicant to tell you about what they did and expound on their experience.

Never put words in the applicant's mouth. Instead of asking, "I see you've had plenty of patient service experience," say, "I see you worked at People's Best Health Clinic. What was that like?"

After they answer, wait an additional five seconds before moving on to the next question. You'll be surprised how many times they add something positive or negative to their prior response that gives you more insight.

Don't ask stray questions that are unrelated to your objectives. Ask questions that will shed light on the applicant in relation to what you're looking for in a new employee.

It's also useful to present the applicant with some hypothetical situations and ask how they would handle them. Make the situations mirror what actually happens in your office, so you can find out what they would do.

It's also useful to present the applicant with some hypothetical situations and ask how they would handle them.

You could also set up a few tests for the applicants. If you're hiring a front desk person, along with a typing test, you might give them a script that details how they should answer the phone and ask the caller pertinent questions. Then you can call the front desk from the back office to see if they follow those directions. Did they ask for the correct spelling of the name? Did they repeat the phone number back to make sure they correctly wrote it down? If the applicant doesn't know how to take a message, do you really want to spend your valuable time training them how to do this?

Now that you've learned about the applicant and their experience, it's time to give them more information about the position. Give them a copy of the job description (always do this after your interview questions, so they don't tailor their answers according to the job description). Tell them what the doctor expects regarding the position. Paint an accurate picture of what the office is like, what the compensation is for the position, and describe potential opportunities for growth.

I've found that it's best to be up front about compensation. During the phone interview, which is the first of three interviews I conduct before we hire someone, I tell potential applicants the hiring wage. You don't want to waste your time with applicants who expect more than the position offers.

Take good notes during the interview, but make them brief because the applicants will get nervous if they see you writing down everything they say. You only need to write down key thoughts or things that will trigger your thoughts about the applicant. It's a good practice to write a summary of what you thought about the applicant immediately after the interview, so you can refresh your memory later.

Now that you have all the information you need from each applicant, it's time to make a decision. You can extend an offer either in person or over the phone. Be sure this person understands the job duties, your expectations, and the compensation—all of which should have been covered during the interview process.

Hiring a new employee isn't easy. The doctor and their practice are in a very vulnerable position. You need to make sure you have everything in order to protect yourself from employment or risk management law suits and to keep the practice running as smoothly as possible during this transition period. Having an employment law attorney on hand was one of the best moves we made in our practice. It saved us from making mistakes that could have cost a lot of money, and it's also given us the peace of mind that we're following all the required state employment laws. I highly recommend that any business owner retain one.

Train for Success—Their Success

It's important that employees have the training and tools they need to be successful in your practice. In a medical office, you'll never be done with training the staff because the systems and procedures are always changing—especially with the way technology is used in the workplace.

When your employees attain their training goals, the practice obtains its goals. Their continued education improves the practice and service you provide to your patients.

It's easy to assume that your employees understand more than they actually do when they're being trained, whether it's their initial job training or if you're training for a new task. Everyone has a different way of learning, and if you don't take the time to ask the employee what they understand as you go along, you can only assume that they've learned what you meant to teach. And you don't want to make assumptions.

> It's easy to assume that your employees understand more than they actually do when they're being trained...

To avoid that, try *coaching* them rather than *training* them. In coaching, you teach them the basics of their job duties first and support that teaching with visual and written protocols.

When they've learned their basic job tasks, go back and review them from time to time to make sure the basics stick.

From the employee's perspective, learning new things can be overwhelming. They might be afraid to ask questions or let you know they don't understand something for fear of seeming inadequate. Start slowly. If they get overwhelmed, they can't retain the information they need to learn to fulfill their responsibilities. Since the threshold of what a person can learn and retain in one session varies, be sure to discuss this with the trainee, so they can let you know how they're doing.

Prepare a notebook that contains the pertinent job tasks protocols and include some blank sheets of paper, so they can take notes during their training and refer back to them later. If they get stuck on the job, they can check their notebook for instructions rather than interrupt another employee to re-teach them. When you break down their duties into clear concepts with specific goals to attain, you set them up for success.

Give them praise and appropriate constructive criticism in equal measure as required. Praise is especially important. When it's necessary to correct, do it in a non-threatening manner. Let them know that your goal is for them to excel in this position, and that it's necessary for them to learn the job tasks correctly.

Create a job task training timeline that includes the job task(s) to be taught, which week that training will take place, and a regular, weekly time to review their training progress. During this time, the employee can demonstrate that they've learned the task. As the employee completes each week's training goals, new ones are scheduled for the following week. This way, your new hire will understand that you're invested in their success and want to establish open communications. That will build their trust in you and foster a good working relationship.

Training and coaching take time and patience, but it's worth it to have happy, successful employees who achieve the goals you've set for them.

Develop an Environment for Continued Training and Teamwork

Building a team of any kind—sports, work, family, or community-related—takes work, and the process of keeping your team together and assuring that everyone's on the same page is an ongoing effort. There are a few key elements that need to be in the mix to develop an A+ team. Be sure to emphasize these key elements:

1. Everyone on the team is expected to lead by example. Great team players don't wait to see how others on the

team perform before they do their part. They jump in feet first, focus on their job tasks, and do the best job they can, so the team will be successful.

2. All team members build relationships with each other and help one another. They take the company's vision and goals and apply them, not only to their position, but they also find ways to help their fellow team members in order to reach the company goals.

3. Team members hold one another accountable. Everyone makes mistakes and great team players recognize this. But they also know when someone is slacking off and needs a nudge to get back in the game and play by the rules.

4. Great team players have positive, contagious attitudes. Their demeanor is positive and uplifting, which fosters good relationships amongst the team.

5. Great team players are humble. They know they're a player on the team just like the others. No superstars allowed. They're open to learning and correction, so the team gets stronger and reaches their goals.

I've had the wonderful opportunity to work on such a team. Over the years, my teammates have been amazing, and I've always felt privileged to work side-by-side with them. Notice that I said *work* with them. This is one of the most important factors of successful teams. Each member needs to see that the manager is working hard the meet the goals of the overall practice and for each person who works there. The employees know it takes work to keep everyone moving forward, and they're willing to do what it takes themselves to help create an A+ team. They've seen that work ethic demonstrated by their manager and they feel that manager's support.

Great Teams Have Great Leaders

There are many layers to creating a great work team, like hiring the right people for positions, having a great work environment, and providing excellent ongoing training.

But there's also an essential top layer, without which no team will be successful. You absolutely, without question, must have a great leader for the team to follow. Without this, the team will always struggle and be mediocre.

Here are five qualities that leader must have:

- Great focus
- Dogged persistence
- Excellent communication skills
- Firm accountability
- High integrity

Great focus: The manager must know the practice's goals and guide the team to reach them. They cannot be wish-washy; they need to be firm in making decisions and giving directions, so each team member can better focus on their own individual tasks.

If the leader can't stay focused and on track, and the direction changes from one day to the next, the staff becomes disillusioned and upset, and they get tired of the game. They stop caring because they don't know what the true focus of the practice is.

Dogged persistence: All great things take time, and building a great work team is no different. Know this and share it with the employees often. No matter what challenges and changes come to the practice, you must persist. If you do, your team will stay by your side.

If you need some inspiration in persistence read *The Slight Edge: Turning Simple Disciplines into Massive Success & Happiness* by Jeff Olson. He states, "It's small daily improvements that are the key to staggering long-term results."

The key word is *daily*. If the manager doesn't go the extra mile every single day, you can't expect that from the staff.

Excellent communication skills: A great leader communicates the practice purpose and vision to the staff. Morning huddles are the perfect way to do this. In these gatherings, the entire office staff discusses what's ahead for the day, the expectations, and any potential complications.

The manager must also listen to the staff, take their input into consideration, and keep an open mind. Great leaders know this game isn't about them; it's about the team and the practice's purpose.

Firm accountability: It's so much easier to blame things on others or on circumstances than it is to hold yourself accountable. But if you play the blame game when something's actually your fault, you're putting blinders on your own eyes while everyone else can see the truth.

No one likes working with someone who won't be accountable for his or her work and behavior. If the leader lacks accountability, it speaks volumes about the practice's standards. Admit your mistakes and faults, then work to correct them. Being vulnerable fosters a climate of cooperation rather than a climate of blame.

High integrity: Always do what's right, no exceptions. Gunnar Lovelace, co-CEO and co-founder of Thrive Market says this:

> Our employees are a direct reflection of the values we embody as leaders. If we are playing from a reactive and obsolete playbook of needing to be right instead of doing what is right, then we limit the full potential of your business and lose quality talent. If you focus on becoming authentic in all your interactions, that will rub off on your business and your culture, and the rest takes care of itself.

Great teams don't happen by chance. They are first carefully selected and are then developed over time with diligent care, training, and inspiration. It takes a great leader to do this.

Chapter 6

The Director's Chair

You become a director by calling yourself a director and you then persuade other people that this is true.
— Peter Brook

ILOVE WATCHING A PERFORMANCE, big or small, because I appreciate the effort that goes into making the performance the best it can be.

As managers, we can perfect the performance in our workplace, which will help our patients experience one of the best medical practices ever.

These four efforts will ensure your team's performance is the best:

- Set the stage
- Create great performers
- Remember that the show must go on
- Master the director's position

If you've ever been in a play or other performance of some sort, what you wanted most was for your audience to love it. In order for that to happen, you had to prepare, rehearse, learn your lines, and master the basics of getting ready for the performance. Before the show, you had butterflies in your stomach, got the jitters, wrung your hands, and rehearsed the show over and over in your mind, wanting to give the best performance possible. It was all about putting yourself out there so others would feel good and enjoy the show, while you reveled in what you were doing.

That's exactly what we do every day in our medical practices; we're putting on a show. We perform our jobs and create value for others. Good performers deliver the best we have, whether it's a "one liner" or we're the main character. We know we're part of whole performance, and we act our part to the best of our ability, so the entire show is the best it can be. We give it our all and then some.

> That's exactly what we do every day in our medical practices; we're putting on a show.

How about you? Do you perform your job the best that it can be done? Do you add value to what you do each day? You can add value by doing more than is necessary and exceeding the expectations of your co-workers, employers, and—most of all—your patients.

Pump up your personality, be enthusiastic about what you're doing, be genuine and enjoy yourself, and others around you will also enjoy you. Meet the needs of your customers, co-workers, and employers in advance. Anticipate what they may need and jump on it. Do what you've always done, but find a way to do it better than you've ever done it before. Take time to think about what you can do to make each day's performance the best you've ever given!

How do you think a Broadway star performs in a show night after night—sometimes the same show for years— but when you see the show, it seems like it was the first time they'd performed it? They have passion for what they do, it's their job, and they love it!

When you walk into your work today, think of it as walking through the backstage door of the theater and prepare yourself for showtime.

Set the Stage: Create a Great Work Environment

As a leader, you can make or break your workplace atmosphere. If you're in a bad mood, everyone else will feel those vibes, and what they feel will show up in their work. They may be quiet, less productive, feel sad, or wish they were doing something other than working with you. Conversely, you have the power to make each day a great one for yourself and the entire team.

I am a 100 percent advocate for happiness at work. I try to promote happiness in our workplace every day. If I had to work with people who expressed oppression and apathy, I couldn't do it.

Of course, your job won't be nirvana, but you can bring happiness and sunshine with you each day. Brendon Burchard is one of my favorite thought leaders. He always says, "Bring the joy!" wherever you go. Whenever he walks through a doorway, he thinks to himself, "bring the joy." What a way to make an entrance and help those you encounter have a great experience with you!

Begin by evaluating your behavior and attitude toward work. Is it good? Do you like what you do? Do you like going to work? When you start by checking yourself, you can make sure you don't enter the workplace with a glass half-empty attitude. The people you work with and for don't deserve that.

People who are generally happy and have a positive attitude tend to be more productive and creative at work. This makes sense because when you feel good and are optimistic, you're more motivated in most areas of life. And that's what employers want. And they want it badly because cheerful, self-motivated people bring many benefits into the workplace. Others naturally gravitate toward happy people; they enjoy being around them because it makes them feel good.

Here are few things that you can do to inspire a culture of happiness:

- Focus on the positive.
- Offer solutions to problems.
- Show your coworkers that you care about them.
- Be an encourager.
- Practice thoughtful actions.
- Smile while you're performing your job duties. Smiling is infectious!

You spend a third of your week at work, a third sleeping, and a third taking care of your personal life. That's a lot of time invested at work, so why don't you make it a happy place to be?

> People who are generally happy and have a positive attitude tend to be more productive and creative at work.

Life has plenty of ups and downs, and they'll certainly have some effect on your work life. But remember that you're being paid to work, and you must give your employer and those you serve your very best, nothing less.

Create Great Performers

If you want to create dedicated and loyal employees, they must first feel valued. It starts on their very first day and doesn't end until their employment has ended.

Try to catch employees doing something good instead of something wrong. Then reward, recognize, and celebrate their good deed to create a culture where the employees flourish.

Ask yourself (or better yet, your work team) the following questions about your office:

- How often does good performance go unrecognized?
- In general, what's the positive-to-negative feedback ratio in this practice?
- How could that ratio be improved?
- What's *your own* individual positive-to-negative feedback ratio to those you manage?
- How can you give your coworkers more positive feedback ?
- What can you do today to show your coworkers that you appreciate them? How can you help change the workplace culture to one where everyone feels appreciated?

One of the deepest of human yearnings is to be appreciated. Businesses that make employee recognition an important part of their culture create loyal employees. By showing appreciation, you not only create a great place to work, you'll feel great about how you make others feel.

Recently, I had a dental appointment. My dentist, whom I've known for several years, thanked me for referring one of our employees to him.

Then the hygienist said, "Your employees seem to really like working in your office, and they seem to stay there for a long time."

"That's good to hear," I said. I told her that many of our employees stay with us for several years. And even when they do move on because they earned a degree or life took them down a different path, we remain friends, and they refer patients to our practice.

My dentist and the hygienist were shocked by that. Then they asked, "How do you keep employees for so long and keep those friendships alive?"

"We try very hard to create a great work environment where our employees can thrive and enjoy themselves," I said. "We learn to play together each day and play nicely. We're professional, but we also have fun. We're all human and have many faults, but we have many more positive attributes that contribute to the practice. We complement each other."

In our office, we're a team. Just as the quarterback has their specific strength, which is different from the guard or tight end, we each bring something necessary to our work each day to share with each other and the patients we serve. Do we have to work at this? Yes, we do, but don't all great teams invest in a lot of hard practice? It also takes a lot of caring and communication, which take time and effort, but the payoff is so worth it.

The Show Must Go On: Focus on the Positives

If doesn't happen today or tomorrow, you can pretty much guarantee that the day after, you'll face some kind of problem at home or work. When it happens at work, you should always be ready to jump in to help with the solution as soon as possible. If you work as a team, you can overcome many obstacles together and continue to offer your patients great service—even when you face challenges.

"Such is life!" is what my Italian grandfather used to say when problems would arise. My grandfather had been through some tough times when he came to America as an immigrant. He learned many lessons during this time, and by the time his grandchildren were growing up, whenever a problem would arise, he'd always smile and laugh. And then he started coming up with ideas to remedy the problem.

> If you work as a team, you can overcome many obstacles together and continue to offer your patients great service—even when you face challenges.

Since there's no way to avoid problems and difficult situations, maybe you should try to do as my grandfather did and take care of the situation as soon as possible. Today we call that creative thinking. He would talk out loud about the many different possibilities of fixing the problem and what the potential outcome might be. After weighing the options, he'd pick a plan and pursue the issue at hand.

There are three important steps you can take when facing personal and professional issues:

1. **Change your focus.** When faced with troubled times, like sick children, financial issues, personal struggles, or if you're just having a bad day, you might tend to focus on your troubles. But how will anything get better if you look inward at the struggle without trying to solve the

problem? The more you focus on your problems, the worse they will seem. Soon, you'll feel overwhelmed.

While you're at work, look outward, think about what you do and how it affects those you work for, those you work with, and the patients you serve. Ask, "What can I do to make their day, their experience, a better one?" When you focus outward, it usually has a positive effect on you, and you begin to lift yourself up from the issues that are weighing you down.

2. **Practice what psychologists call *reframing*.** Is the cup half empty or half full? Are you an optimist or a pessimist? If you were planning on taking the kids to the park to play, but it started to rain, do you get upset and say, "The rain has ruined our day. Now we can't go to the park." Or do you look at the situation and say, "Since we have rain, let's have fun making a tent in the house or baking cookies."

   Reframe the negative by finding something positive to replace it. Take on the challenge. You'll be so glad you did.

3. **Make a happy thought list.** This is a list of things that make you happy. Take the time to jot down the big and little things that make you happy and bring a smile to your face. Maybe it's watching your children play, or it's a favorite childhood memory. When it comes to you, write down that memory or put up pictures of your children around you. Then when you're down, you can look at your happy thought list and be uplifted. You always have a choice about how you look at situations. Make the decision to do something positive when you're facing difficulty. It will only benefit you and those you work with.

Remember that *the show must go on,* and your paying customers never need to know the struggles you deal with personally or professionally.

Mastering the Director's Chair

Whether you use the term coaching, managing, or supervising, if you don't do it with your people in mind, then you may not be the right person for the job. That may sound harsh, but keep reading before you make any critical judgments.

You work for the practice owner and have been entrusted to instruct, guide, and inspire the staff. It's what your job description states, and it's what is expected.

Here are three small words that encompass your responsibilities, which are simple but difficult for several reasons;

- **Instruct:** Your job is to instruct. But not all people learn the same way or at the same rate. During training, you may need to adopt different teaching methods to ensure that everyone's playing on the same field and understands the game plan. Some players may catch on quickly and others may take longer. Instructing is not a one-size-fits-all task. You need to understand this and be trained in how to teach the same tasks in a variety of ways.

- **Guide:** You job is to guide. When your employees have learned the basics of their job positions, you'll have to continue to guide them—or come alongside them—on that path, so they will focus and help make the practice productive. Each employee will respond to a different type of guidance. Some will accept that this is what needs to take place as you determine what they're capable of learning. Others won't want to be guided and will want to step out on their own when they've been fully trained. The same method won't work for all employees.

- **Inspire:** You job is to inspire, which is probably the hardest of the three tasks to execute and continue to do. What inspires one person may not inspire another. You have to get to know the people you supervise and understand what makes them tick, so you can continue to light the fire and inspire them to keep them going strong.

It's not easy to lead employees. It takes understanding, patience, and commitment to them. You might get frustrated with your staff members if they don't respond as quickly as you'd like in one of the areas listed above. When this happens, it's not uncommon to form false conclusions and to let them go, when they simply need to be coached in a different way. Don't make that mistake.

If you're called to lead, coach, manage or supervise, these simple rules will help you be the kind of leader your staff will respect and respond to:

1. Great coaches rally the whole team together. Coaches don't rally only a few members of the team; they rally them all.

2. Great coaches believe all team members are equal, even though their jobs are different. Don't play favorites or create superstars, as you will be creating your own problems.

3. Great coaches realize that mistakes reveal lessons to be learned whether the team member or the coach makes the mistake.

4. Great coaches put their team members first and don't throw anyone under the bus.

5. Great coaches realize that they're working with people, not widgets.

6. Great coaches ask team members questions and allow them to form their own answers and actions.

There are so many great examples of coaches that you can read about and from whom you can gain valuable insight. Vince Lombardi, John Wooden, Pat Riley, and Phil Jackson are just a few. There are books about each of them that are worth reading if you're in a coaching/managing position.

When a great coach is leading the team, each person will be able to say that they feel valued. This is something that you must strive for to be successful in serving your team. If the people you work with say that they're valued by you, then you are valuable to them.

My Mom, the Great Director

When I was a young girl, my mother had a list of chores that each of my siblings and I needed to complete each Saturday morning while she was at the beauty shop. When I was really young, I had to take out the trash, fold some clothes, and pick up my room.

> When a great coach is leading the team, each person will be able to say that they feel valued.

My sister, who was older, got to clean the bathrooms; I couldn't wait until I was old enough to do this glorious job. Then the day came when I graduated to cleaning the bathrooms, and my mother, who was a smart woman and a great director, took time to show me in detail what needed to be done and how she expected it to look when I was finished. I knew that my job would be inspected when she got home.

I really wanted to please my mom, so I tried really hard to get it right the first time, but I missed a few things. When she got home, she had no problem letting me know what I hadn't done to her specifications. She took the time to watch me do the tasks until I could perform them properly. She'd set a standard and it needed to be upheld.

Over time, I was able to get those bathrooms clean and pass the inspection with flying colors, but even though I could do a good job, my mother still would look it over to make sure I hadn't slacked off. My mother was instilling in me good work habits that I took with me through my whole life, and I thank her for this now.

So, what does a child's chores have to do with working in a medical office? Good management personnel need to be the director for their employees in the same way that my mother was for my siblings and me. You need to hold your employees to your performance standards.

In addition to clearly communicating the job expectations, you need to demonstrate how you expect the tasks to be performed. Have training sheets with itemized tasks and goals for each employee to reference and follow. Take time to show them what a good job looks like and set that as the expectation.

By having directions and inspections for each task, you can ensure that the job is done correctly. Your employees will be happier because they'll know what's expected from them and you will be happier because the standard has been set and taught.

Another reason to have tasks and directions written down is that when something does fall through the cracks, you can ask the staff member to review their training sheet to get back in line with your expectations.

Learn to be a director. The director is in charge of making all the components of a play run smoothly. They're in charge of pre-production, the actual production, and post-production. They don't do the work, but oversee it.

The actors will either love or hate the director depending on how they're treated and if they feel valued. To make sure you're a loved director, at the end of each day ask yourself, "Would I have liked being directed by me?"

Chapter 7

Handling Challenges

*The heart that gives thanks is a happy one,
for we cannot feel thankful and unhappy
at the same time.*
~ Douglas Wood

ONE OF THE BIGGEST CHALLENGES of being a manager is working with people. When you work with people, you're going to have people problems. That's just a fact of life, and it's true at home and at work.

The key to working with people is to take a step back and refrain from reacting before you've asked some questions, especially when a challenging situation presents itself. Otherwise, you might think you understand what's going on and react inappropriately when what you thought was happening is not the case at all.

Because I don't always know what's happened or understand the other person's point of view, I ask simple questions like, "Did I understand you to say . . . " or, "Can you explain what happened, so I can understand better?" These questions have saved me from creating many potential problems.

You'd be surprised at how often my first impressions are wrong and how often I've misunderstood a situation. Also, just because we're all adults, it doesn't mean that we always act like it, as the following story reminded me.

Our Visitor

A few years ago, a high school student wanted to shadow our team as we worked. Kacey came prepared with plenty of questions for me about managing the office. She wanted to know what I liked best and what were my challenges. The summer before, she'd worked an internship in a large hospital system. She was curious if we ever experienced co-worker conflict in our office, and if so, what we did about it.

She said that kind of conflict was a problem where she'd done her internship, and they had a couple of meetings to address issues between staff members.

"That was really an eye-opener to me," she said. "I never knew adults would behave like that at work. They talked about each other behind their backs, and some of them were pretty tough on the others."

It brought back memories of when I graduated high school and first started working at a financial institution. I, too, was shocked to learn that there was quite a bit of gossip and backbiting between the staff members. I didn't know that adults ever acted that way.

I told Kacey that, at times, we'd had employees who tried to stir the pot between co-workers, but that our policy was to have open communications with each other. If there were any issues, we worked through them face-to-face.

"Even though working people are all adults," I explained, "it doesn't mean they know how to get along and communicate well with one another. Plus, there can be personality conflicts. But if the manager's on top of things, they'll work hard to create an environment that discourages this type of behavior."

I said that in our office, we all admit when we've made a mistake. It's just a fact of life; mistakes happen. Taking responsibility for the mistakes you made, working to make things right, and trying not to repeat the mistake was important in our office. Kacey liked that we valued honesty, ethics, and integrity. She could see that the workplace is much better when you can trust everyone.

> ... in our office, we all admit when we've made
> a mistake.

She shadowed our other staff members to learn about their job duties and learned that it takes a team that works well together to make a practice successful. I loved listening to the answers our staff members gave when Kacey asked them the same questions she'd asked me. There was a common foundation in all our answers, and I heard them voice how we were all bonded together by our office culture. It was clear that everyone wanted to make this practice one where we loved to work every day and one where our patients loved to come when they needed us.

That evening, Kacey's mom called to thank me for letting her shadow us. She said that Kacey really liked our office and was excited about how we all really enjoyed our work, our patients, and each other.

The funny thing is that I think we got more out of having Kacey there than she did. Her visit inspired us to continue to work hard to maintain our healthy, strong work environment. It was clear that we were proud to share what we'd accomplished with someone new.

Cultivating Resilience

When changes are happening in the workplace and you don't know how things will end up, you can allow yourself to get uptight and stressed. During tough times, you need to develop resilience.

According to Oxford Languages, the definition of resilient is: (1) able to withstand or recover quickly from difficult conditions, (2) able to recoil or spring back into shape after bending, stretching, or being compressed.

When I think of being resilient, I think about soldiers. When in battle, soldiers live on autopilot, ready to face the unknown every day. They need to be flexible, tough, durable, strong, and quick to recover, so they can do it again day after day.

If you're resilient in your work life, you're usually successful in most aspects of your life. To be resilient, you need to embrace the three Cs—commitment, control, and challenge—so you can withstand disaster, devastation, or derailing.

Commitment: When you make a commitment, you dedicate yourself to something, perhaps a person, cause, or job. It's important to consider the cost before you make a commitment because a commitment obligates you to do something.

Control: Control is the power to direct your own behavior, influence other people's behavior, and—potentially—the course of events. As a manager, you must control yourself but also realize that you have great influence over others and outcomes. A manager must always use control to better the practice and the people who work there.

Challenge: Everyday managers are faced with varying work or employee situations, large and small, that call for them to put on their thinking caps. To be successful in finding solutions for these situations, they must be able to handle the pressure and immediate attention these instances may require, which can be frustrating if their own job tasks are interrupted. These day-to-day problems can be challenging and managers must be up to this type of challenge, which is a component of the position.

> If you're resilient in your work life,
> you're usually successful in most aspects of your life.

Resilience is not an inherent trait; it can be learned and mastered. When working with and managing people, keep the three Cs in your tool bag. You'll need them on a daily basis while you're working in the trenches.

Address Issues Immediately

Whenever your employees have questions, concerns, or problems, be sure to address them as soon as possible. I learned this the hard way by thinking that if I just ignored or lightly mentioned a problem but didn't resolve it, that it would eventually go away.

But ignoring things didn't work out so well with one of the first staff members I hired. She was just out of college, and this was her first real job in a medical office. She was a fast learner and did her job well. The problem was her temper. She would get mad at the slightest issue: if a patient was late, if she had to wait on the phone too long to verify insurance benefits, or if I asked her to do something that she didn't expect to do. I wasn't sure how to handle this situation and neither was the doctor. So, I'd talk about bringing our best self to work and that we should put on our "happy faces" when we walked in the door. One day she got mad and didn't talk to me all day. I said that people couldn't build relationships and work well together unless they talk to one another.

None of this seemed to help. She'd go a couple of weeks without an outburst or giving me the silent treatment and then—BAM!—it would happen again, usually when I was the only one around. She never did this in front of the doctor.

One day, she exploded about all the charting she had to file. I'd had enough. I said, "One more outburst, and I'll have to let you go."

She just stared at me. I was proud that I'd finally gave her a warning, but within minutes I was on the phone with the police because she threw something at me.

I stood up and said, "You're fired. Get out of this office now."

She spat out, "You better watch your back because I'll get you, and you won't even know what hit you."

I let the police know about the threat, and I felt like I was going to faint. My knees were shaking and my head was spinning. But I learned a lesson: be clear when you need to deal with an issue, deal with it quickly, and don't let it get out of hand.

If you put off employee issues, you risk creating a bigger, more complex problem, or even losing a valued employee. You're likely to have this problem until you learn how to manage your people and the situations that arise, such as in the case below that turned out differently than my situation.

> If you put off employee issues, you risk creating a bigger, more complex problem, or even losing a valued employee.

Anna struggled to keep up with the workload assigned to her. She felt overwhelmed, stressed, and undertrained. She told her manager that her workload was too much and she needed additional training. He said he'd discuss it with her later when he had more time.

Several days went by and Anna heard nothing from her manager. She didn't want to bother him because she knew he was busy, but she was falling further behind in her work. It was making her stressed and physically ill.

Anna saw the manager in the break room and reminded him that she needed to discuss her workload problem. She said that she was concerned because every day she fell further and further behind.

He patted her on the back and said, "Do the best you can. We all have a lot to do, and we'll eventually get caught up."

The stress was too much for Anna and she quit. When her manager was questioned about why she left without giving notice, he said, "She wasn't the right person for the job."

How could he possibly think that? He never took the time to listen to Anna to find out about the problem.

If you turn a deaf ear to your employee's questions or complaints, you'll have a high turnover. The reason they ask you questions or tell you their complaints is to get your help. That's one of the reasons you're there, right?

If you take the time to listen to your employee's issues and address them, it shows that you value them and their concerns. Most employee *questions* can be answered quickly, but very few employee *issues* require fast action. The issues need to first be acknowledged. Then give the employee a time frame for discussing and resolving the problem.

An employer's most important—and expensive—assets are their employees. Take the time to listen and resolve their issues; it's quite costly if you do not.

> Take the time to listen and resolve their issues;
> it's quite costly if you do not.

Challenges of Employee Conflict

Are Sue and Annie at it again? You can always tell because the desk drawers close a little harder, the phone is hung up more abruptly, and there's tension in the air. What happened this time?

All workplaces have some sort of conflict between co-workers or staff and management at one time or another. Whenever people work together, there will be people issues. It's best to know this up front and find ways to work through the issues that arise.

But you don't have to be caught off guard. Before things get out of hand, develop a conflict resolution policy that all employees are expected to honor. Openly discuss the policy so that everyone understands how it works. Then ask each employee to sign a statement that they've read the policy, understand it, and will adhere it.

Here are some suggestions:

1. Write a policy that details how complaints will be submitted and handled. If the complaint is between employees,

for example, one of them would go to the manager or business owner for resolution. If the problem is between an employee and their manager, the employee would go to the person to whom the manager reports. It's critical that the order of escalation is clear to everyone.

2. All complaints or issues must be submitted in writing and include a possible solution for the problem. People tend to take more time to think through an issue when they write it down, and sometimes they realize the issue can be handled without involving a manager. But if a manager's attention is required, they'll need a day to think about it and understand the issue before taking any action.

3. The manager must respond to all complaints within twenty-four to forty-eight hours (or sooner if someone could be injured or is being threatened). All parties involved should be given a chance to share their view. The best way to resolve an issue is to bring all parties together to discuss the issue and possible ways to resolve it in a non-threatening environment. Give them all the facts and be sure they have time to prepare for the meeting.

4. The ultimate goal is to resolve the issue so it doesn't happen again. The fastest way to resolution is to be sure you have the correct information first so that you understand the problem and can determine possible solutions.

5. There are several other factors to consider, such as how many times the same issue has occurred; if you've given any previous warnings; if the parties involved are willing to work through the issue in a positive way; if there were any threats, discriminations, or abuse. Certain issues cannot be tolerated, and you need to make sure you know your state laws, so you can take the correct steps for the protection of all involved and without recourse to your employer.

If you have a process for handling conflict professionally and quickly, you'll have fewer interruptions to the business.

Picking Yourself Up

Every day won't be your best, and at times, you may find yourself stuck in a rut. Perhaps you feel down or sorry for yourself, and you just can't seem to pull out of it. Your feelings may have been triggered by a challenging event or an unhappy change in your life. But if you can't pick yourself up and move through the issue, it can become serious, possibly requiring outside help to recover.

My friend Rita was in such a time in her life. She was in a rut. She'd been transferred to a new department at work and wasn't happy about the change. Instead of embracing it and getting to know her new coworkers, she became resentful and withdrawn.

Her husband wanted to help her. He'd recently embraced a new challenge, and he thought it might help her too. Rita had wanted to get new flooring for their house, and until now he'd held off. But he knew it would be worth the purchase if she would try to do the grateful challenge.

The challenge was to identify three things that she was grateful for every day for a period of twenty-one days. Rita was to write down those three things and tell them to her family each night at dinner. She not only had to tell them what she was grateful for, but why. Rita jumped at the challenge because she really wanted new flooring.

To make a long story short, she not only got her new floors, but during the process she became grateful for her new job and coworkers. About two weeks into the challenge, Rita came home and told her family about how much she was enjoying her new job.

I think this was one smart husband. I also think that this challenge is brilliant, and you don't have to be in a rut to take it on. How much better would your life be if you did this challenge every day?

I've made a habit of picking one to three things that I'm grateful for each day. I pronounce these things out loud and then say why I'm grateful for them. I do the grateful challenge when I'm driving to work because it makes me realize how fortunate I am for that day, and it puts me in the right mindset before I get to the office.

> I've made a habit of picking one to three things that I'm grateful for each day.

I've also made it a habit to read from a good, uplifting book every day. I read for my own personal growth, and I'm convinced that this one habit has made a huge impact on who I am and how I think. I have an extensive library, and I re-read sections from various books when situations come up that pertain to that problem. I also listen to audio books or watch motivational thought leaders while I'm on my treadmill three times a day. (Yes, I walk nearly seven miles a day, six days a week. I'm on the treadmill morning, noon and evening!) If you feed your mind with good, positive input every day, good and positive things will flow from you to others.

You have a choice in how you present yourself to others, and when set yourself up for success each day with a positive mindset, it makes a difference in every encounter you have.

Chapter 8

You Are the Winner!

Motivation is the art of getting people to do what you want them to do because they want to do it.
~ Dwight D. Eisenhower

MOST OF THE LEADERSHIP management training I've received emphasizes how important it is to praise your team members. When you compliment your employees, it increases their self-worth and inspires them to do a great job. Less frequently discussed is how important it is to train your employees to pass that praise along. In an ideal workplace, the team not only compliments their coworkers, but their patients, vendors, and delivery people.

Not long ago, one of our patients who was moving out of state came in for her last appointment. During this visit, she told the medical assistant, "You have the best medical office that I've ever been in. You run on time, everyone's always very pleasant and helpful. You always make me feel important and cared for. I can tell you all enjoy your jobs. I will miss coming to your office." The positive effect of this compliment was a tremendous boost for all of us.

How nice that this woman took the time to tell us how she felt about the care and service we offered. It made us all feel good about what we did, and it reinforced the value of striving to do better each day. And we—every single member of the team—can do the same for every person we encounter during the business day.

Here are a few examples of how your team can make people feel appreciated:

- A company from which you purchase supplies does a great job with your order. It arrives to you on time. Now I know this is expected, but what if you gave the manager of the company a quick call and told them what a good job Bob did with your order and that you appreciate it. How do you think Bob will feel when he hears that you called?

- You discovered a mistake on a bill. You call the vendor. One of their staff figures it out and fixes the problem. You can not only thank this person on the phone but also send a thank you card or an email as a follow-up for helping you.

- The toilet broke in the office. The landlord sent someone over right away to fix it. Yes, it's their job to do this, but let them know you appreciate that they cared about and resolved the problem right away. This will make them feel great about what they do.

- Say thank you and have a great day to the mail person, UPS, or FedEx person, the person who delivers the drinking water, etc.

- Thank your patients for coming to your place of business. Let them know you appreciate them. Tell them that it's people like them who make your business successful. It takes so little, yet it means so much, when you let others know you appreciate them, what they do for you, and the business you work for.

Let Others Know You Appreciate Them and What They Do

At the end of a recent trip to Italy, my hand luggage didn't clear the airport security scanner. I was pulled aside to have my bag searched by a young inspector. I felt terrible because I'm a frequent flyer and know what not to have in my bag. I remembered that one of the wineries I visited had given me a bottle opener, and I forgot to remove it before packing. I told him what he'd find, but I wasn't allowed to help him.

He kept searching until he found it. He'd worked up a sweat, and I had the feeling he was pretty new at his job. Upon bringing the opener out of the bag, I said, "That was a great job."

He looked at me in amazement and said, "Signora, no one has ever thanked me for what I do. They usually are very angry with me."

I told him that he should be thanked, he did his job very well, and I appreciated it.

A few words of praise can make a difference in someone else's day because they need to hear that what they do is important to you. What does it cost to say something positive and nice to someone? Nothing—it's free! Give as much of it away as possible each day. It will not only make a difference to those you encounter and in your place of employment, it will also change your life. Take the appreciation challenge today:

see how many people you can thank or compliment while at work today.

> A few words of praise can make a difference in some-
> one else's day because they need to hear that what
> they do is important to you.

Businesses depend on people. Whether it's customers, pa-tients, clients, or coworkers, they all deserve to receive the best service you can give each day. How you serve your clients or coworkers can make a big difference in how they feel, not only about you but about the business.

Since you're in the service business, you should always give your best service. Ask yourself these five questions and then rate yourself from 1-5, with 1 being poor, 2 average, 3 good, 4 very good, and 5 excellent. Then tally up your answers to get your service skills score:

1. Am I friendly all the time?
2. Do I stay positive all the time?
3. Do I make it easy to do business with my company and me?
4. Do I work well with my coworkers?
5. Do I empathize with customers or coworkers when they have a problem and try to help them?

It may be hard to score a 5 on everything each day. But you can greatly increase customer and coworker satisfaction by trying to be the best you can every day. Evaluating yourself with those questions on a regular basis is a good place to start.

Becoming my best self is a lifelong project, one that I need to work on every day. Just when I've achieved one of my goals and think I can take it easy, I realize that I still have a long way to go. There's no arrival date; it's a constant work in progress with millions of baby steps each year.

Here are some questions to ask yourself in regard to your personal development:

- Do I know where I'm headed?
- Do I have specific goals and dreams?
- Do I have a plan to achieve those goals and dreams?

Time is precious, and it's easily wasted if you do nothing to move forward. If you don't have a weekly plan, start one now and then set up a specific time each week to review how you did and what you still need to do. Life is a gift. Don't waste any of it.

Called to Lead

People often think they can't be a leader unless someone gives them the title. This is simply not true. If you believe you're called to be a leader and helping others achieve their best potential is your passion, then you will do it.

A title is just a title. Being a leader is who you *are*, and it's demonstrated through the attributes you display. Leaders hunger to be the best they can be. Leaders breed leaders. They don't walk ahead of their team. They bring their team alongside them, and eventually they move to the back of the pack where they joyfully watch their people move forward to become leaders themselves.

In the *Harvard Business Review Guide to Motivating People: Engage Your Employees, Energize Your Team, Boost Performance*, the authors address what makes a good, successful manager. They discuss what they call *the power factor* and assert that the most successful managers have this power factor.

This caused me to lift an eyebrow at first because, as a manager, I never liked the thought of having power. My management style is to coach my team, and the word *power* always seemed negative to me. But after reading the book, I had a whole new understanding about having power as a manager and what it means to possess it in a positive way.

The power factor means that you powerfully motivate your employees. Quoting from the book, "Remember that the term, 'power motivation' refers not to dictatorial behavior but to a desire to have an impact, to be strong and influential." The authors found that the better managers possessed this power factor and the morale of their people was higher, their relationships were better, and they produced more. Now that's a power I definitely want to have over my team!

> The power factor means that
> you powerfully motivate your employees.

The managers who had this power were ones who really cared for their people and about their needs. It excited me to think that I could have the power to motivate my people to do a better job simply by showing them how much I cared for them. How hard could that be?

Well, apparently it's pretty hard. In the book, they also address how many of the surveyed managers didn't have the power factor. Instead, they were motivated by personal power. Managers who had the power factor created employees who were loyal to the company and saw the company's worth and value. But managers who were motivated by personal power raised employees who were only loyal to them, not to the business. The problem arises when the manager leaves or gets promoted. The people who had been motivated by their personal power didn't fare well, and many of them would leave the company. The opposite was true for those whose manager had the power factor. When their manager moved on, they stayed because they were loyal to the company.

Think about what you're instilling in your team. Are you strengthening their ties to the company? Or is it all about you?

A Growth Mindset

When you hire new employees, do you look for the person who has the best skills or experience? That's not a bad thing, but be sure to find out whether or not the candidate is open to a growth mindset. Managers who have a fixed mindset believe they're hiring people to simply do a job and nothing more. They think that employees are dispensable if they don't work out.

According to Carol S. Dweck, Ph.D., author of *Mindset: The New Psychology of Success*, "Managers with a growth mindset think it's nice to have skilled and talented employees but that is just the starting point. These managers are more committed to their employees' development as well as their own. They give a great deal more developmental coaching, they notice improvement in employees' performance, and they welcome critiques from their employees."

When you make this type of investment in your employees, they grow. They also become more invested in the company. They know you care about them and that their input matters to you.

Growth mindset managers are committed to their own growth as well. Without it, they are just another manager who struggles with the day-to-day tasks of doing a job rather than thriving in a career they're passionate about.

Which type of manager would you want to work with? Which type of manager are you?

> Growth mindset managers are committed
> to their own growth as well.

Peter Drucker was known as "the father of modern management." He wrote multiple books on management and believed it was how people worked together in organizations that made the magic happen, no matter the size.

He found that successful businesses had managers that followed many of the same basic foundational practices.

- They asked, "What needs to be done," not, "What do I want to do."
- They strived together to do what was right for the business.
- When they figured out what was right, they developed actions plans to get it done.
- They took responsibility for the decisions they made, collectively and individually.
- They also took responsibility for their communication with one another as they worked together.
- They focused on opportunities rather than problems.

Individually, each of the above can be easily accomplished, yet many times, it doesn't happen. As the manager, it's up to you to set an example and practice these things. You can raise the standards at work. Not only will your workplace benefit, but you will personally benefit by knowing that you bring and do your best each day.

When you get up in the morning, you decide who you will bring to work. Make it the best you. During the day if you get derailed and start heading down the wrong track, choose to change your mindset and redirect yourself back to high standard and actions. No excuses. Just do it. It's a minute-by-minute choice. Choose to make good choices and be an example for the others in your office.

Chapter 9

The Shift Moment

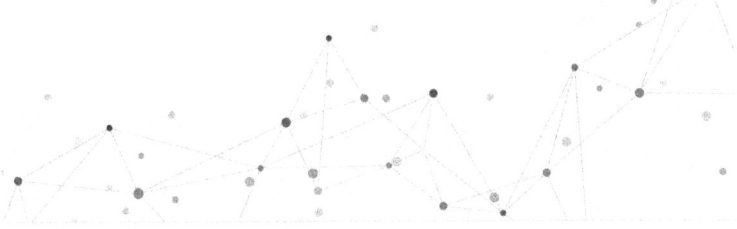

Leadership is a mindset that shifts from being a victim to creating results.
Any one of us can demonstrate leadership in our work and within our lives.
~ Robin S. Sharma

SEVERAL YEARS AGO, I attended a conference with two of my favorite people, my Aunt Dollie and my cousin Sheree. The conference was held at the Sofia Institute in South Carolina. Our main reason for making this trip was to hear Sue Monk Kidd, author of *The Secret Life of Bees*, and her daughter, Ann Kidd Taylor, speak. They are friends of my Aunt Dollie, which made it even more special when my cousin and I had the opportunity to meet and talk with them.

They had just published a book they co-authored together called *Traveling with Pomegranates*. It's a wonderful mother/

daughter story. The book is about their individual quests to redefine themselves and their relationship with each other. I found it very hard to put the book down; it was quite moving because it was the true story of their adventure. They were very transparent and honest with their feelings as they were on this life journey, and they shared it openly in this beautiful book.

During their journey, each of them reaches a point where they arrive at their *shift moment,* the moment when the lights came on; their purpose became clear to each of them, yet individually. They realized their new path and found the strength to pursue it. I found the book both inspiring and uplifting.

Shift moments can happen unexpectedly or as a result of searching for them.

Have you ever had a shift moment? Do you remember what it felt like? I do. Mine was unexpected: the first time I was diagnosed with breast cancer. I was waiting to find out what type of cancer I had and how advanced it was. That moment is as clear to me now as it was twenty-two years ago.

I realized that life is short, and none of us knows how much time we've been given. I knew I had to make the most of my life no matter how long I was here. I wanted to help others learn the beauty of living in the moment and looking for the lessons to be learned in each encounter we have, making our encounters with others memorable for them.

The past twenty-two years have been an adventure. Time passes so quickly; one tends to forget the uncertainties as we forge through the challenges that come our way. I cherish my shift moment. It gave direction to my life's quest. You never know what's in store for you, and I believe that you need to face each day looking for the best and being your best.

> ... living in the moment and looking for the lessons to be learned in each encounter we have, making our encounters with others memorable for them.

Then one day a few years ago, I faced another challenge. I was diagnosed with breast cancer a second time. Although the threat had always been in the back of my mind, it rocked my being to the core when it happened, but it strengthened the foundation of my shift moment. I see much clearer now, living, caring, and bringing joy into each day.

This second diagnosis strengthened my reason for being and my calling to teach, coach, and help others make the best of each day for those at work and those at home.

Each day we are creating our legacy. It's what we invest in others—whether it's at home, at work, or out in the world— that will speak the loudest about who we are and were.

I know what path I am to follow. I hope my journey is a long one because I have a lot to learn, but I enjoy each day as I move through it. As my Aunt Dollie would say, "Life is for those that show up." I'm going to show up each day and do what I'm called to do.

I'm pursuing what my shift moment showed me. Are you?

Only you who can decide whether you'll be a winner or not. And you determine that by each choice you make.

About the Author

TINA DEL BUONO has been a practice manager for over twenty-three years and has worked alongside her husband, Dr. John Hollander, in his practice in Santa Rosa, California.

She has lectured nationally for the past two decades on practical practice management, leadership, and motivational topics for physicians, office managers, and medical staff.

She is a performance management coach and consultant with Top Practices Practice Management, as well as in her own business, Practical Practice Management. She specializes in complete practice efficiencies, team building, staffing issues, physician/staff communications, and manager mentoring.

Tina has written over four hundred articles on practice management, and she's been blogging on management and leadership topics for ten years. Her goal is to provide content that will help the reader continue to grow, learn, change their mindset, and excel, so they can become a better person and make a positive influence in their relationships at work and life.

She has three adult children who are married and have given her four granddaughters, who are the joy of her life. She also loves travels to Italy, the home of their family, with her Aunt Dollie each year.

www.ingramcontent.com/pod-product-compliance
Lightning Source LLC
Chambersburg PA
CBHW071419210326
41597CB00020B/3579